Enterprise Risk Management

Enterprise Risk Management

Bevan Lloyd

Chartered Accountants Ireland

Published by
Chartered Accountants Ireland
Chartered Accountants House
47–49 Pearse Street
Dublin 2
www.charteredaccountants.ie

© The Institute of Chartered Accountants in Ireland 2010

Copyright in this publication is owned by the Institute of Chartered Accountants in Ireland. All rights reserved. No part of this text may be reproduced or transmitted or communicated to the public in any form or by any means, including photocopying, Internet or e-mail dissemination, without the written permission of the Institute of Chartered Accountants in Ireland. Such written permission must also be obtained before any part of this document is stored in a retrieval system of any nature.

This publication is designed to provide accurate and authoritative information in regard to the subject matter covered. It is provided on the understanding that the Institute of Chartered Accountants in Ireland is not engaged in rendering professional services. The Institute of Chartered Accountants in Ireland disclaims all liability for any reliance placed on the information contained within this publication and recommends that if professional advice or other expert assistance is required, the services of a competent professional should be sought.

ISBN: 978-1-907214-33-2

Typeset by Datapage
Printed by ColourBooks

To Maria, Saoirse and Oisín

Contents

Chapter 1	Introduction	1
Chapter 2	**Enterprise Risk Management**	4
	Introduction	4
	Corporate Governance	4
	Definition of 'Enterprise Risk Management'	5
	The Goal of Enterprise Risk Management	7
	The Scope of Enterprise Risk Management	7
	Conclusion	9
Chapter 3	**What is Risk?**	10
	Introduction	10
	Definition of Risk	10
	Likelihood and Impact	11
	'Upside' Risk	12
	Categories of Risk	13
	Emerging Risks	15
	Interaction between Risks	16
	Conclusion	16
Chapter 4	**Required Control Infrastructure**	17
	Introduction	17
	Corporate Vision Statement	17
	Codes of Conduct	20
	Fraud Policy	25
	Reporting Mechanisms	28
	Organisational Charts	31
	Group or Company Policies	32
	Conclusion	36
Chapter 5	**Organisational Structures of Risk Management**	37
	Introduction	37
	Executive Sponsorship	37

	Organisational Structure	38
	Roll-out of the Process	41
	Communication	42
	Recommendations	45
	Embedding the Process	48
	Conclusion	48
Chapter 6	**The Risk Management Process**	**49**
	Introduction	49
	Identifying Risk	49
	Grading Risk	63
	Accepting Risk	72
	Aggregating Risk	78
	Controlling Risk	85
	Updating Risk	89
	Conclusion	93
Chapter 7	**Verifying Controls and Strategies**	**94**
	Introduction	94
	Allocating Controls	94
	Tracking Strategies	95
	'Walkthroughs' of Controls	100
	Monitoring of Controls	103
	Reliance on the Work of Others	108
	Conclusion	109
Chapter 8	**Disaster Recovery**	**110**
	Introduction	110
	Disaster Recovery Plan	111
	Disaster Recovery Team	113
	Scenario Planning	117
	Conclusion	124
Chapter 9	**Fraud Considerations**	**125**
	Introduction	125
	Definition of Fraud	125
	'Tone at the Top'	127
	Fraud Risk Assessment	129

	Legislation	139
	Conclusion	140
Chapter 10	**Challenges and Barriers**	**141**
	Introduction	141
	The Expectation Gap	141
	Engagement from Local Management	142
	Conclusion	148
Index		**149**

Chapter 1

Introduction

The areas of corporate governance in general and enterprise risk management in particular have been receiving increased attention as a result of the current economic upheavals. Various stakeholders, including investors, employees and government, are questioning how some organisations could engage in certain activities without necessarily appreciating, let alone mitigating, the risks associated with them. These failures to understand and manage risk have resulted in spectacular financial losses, losses of confidence and the forced replacement of senior executives.

There are also continuing calls for additional oversight by regulators to ensure that some organisations are, in effect, saved from themselves. Even for those organisations that have survived the recession intact, their traditional business models might have been extensively disrupted, resulting in the emergence of new and unfamiliar risks that now have to be managed. In this context of unprecedented economic difficulty, it is therefore perhaps inevitable that organisations will review and reconsider the effectiveness of their corporate governance and risk management programmes. And this should be done not only to avoid the mistakes of the past, but also as part of planning for the future.

This book aims to provide an overview of enterprise risk management as well as a guide to its implementation. It is anticipated that **senior management** should find this guide helpful as either a blueprint or source of suggestions for maintaining and enhancing their current programmes and controls. Similarly, **non-executive directors** should find it useful as a framework against which to compare the existing risk management programmes of the organisations on whose boards they sit.

Whereas corporate governance models and guidance tends to change from time to time and across jurisdictions, the principles that support enterprise risk management are considerably more stable and consistent. They are, therefore, as applicable to large, listed multinationals as to privately-owned companies.

In **Chapters 2** and **3** we will first describe how enterprise risk management relates to and interacts with the broader corporate governance principles, and then define the various key terms such as 'risk', 'likelihood' and 'impact' that will be used throughout the rest of the text. We will also suggest a number of ways in which these terms can be stratified further into more precise definitions. These suggestions can, of course, be adjusted or re-defined to be useful to a particular organisation and in order align with its ethos and stage of development.

Chapters 4 and **5** will discuss the infrastructure, such as a code of conduct and authorisation matrix, which would form part of the building blocks underpinning an enterprise risk management programme. We will also discuss the alternative organisational structures that an organisation might adopt when implementing such a programme. It is important to note that although this book generally refers to a separate risk management department, other existing structures such as internal audit or the general finance community might be equally suited to oversee the implementation of the enterprise risk management programme, depending on the nature of the particular organisation.

In **Chapters 6** and **7** we will describe in detail the general risk management process, its various phases and how these might be formally implemented by an organisation. Again, whereas the scope of the text assumes a large, diversified and geographically spread organisation, it is by no means exclusively applicable to multinationals. Any organisation where, by virtue of its size or complexity of its business or businesses, executive management is removed from the day-to-day operations should consider a more formalised enterprise risk management programme. Thus, throughout the book, 'business unit' refers not only to a separate legal entity, but can also refer to a department or even an individual function within a company, depending on the nature of the organisation. We will also catalogue some typical examples of the risks expected to be applicable to most organisations as well as suggest the mitigating strategies and controls that might be implemented in response.

Chapters 8 and **9** focus on two particularly 'hot' topics, namely **disaster recovery** and **fraud risk management**. We will examine the areas that a disaster recovery plan should address in general, as well as providing some scenario planning for common disasters such as the incapacity of the warehouse facilities, administrative buildings and IT servers. We will also describe the various fraud risks facing the typical organisation and what responses management might adopt in response. We will then tie these back to the requirements of the new UK Bribery Act. This legislation will be of particular importance to Irish companies operating on an all-island basis or that have subsidiaries in Britain.

Chapter 10 concludes the book in discussing some of the usual challenges and barriers that an organisation might encounter during the implementation of a formalised enterprise risk management programme. Possible responses or alternative approaches that could be considered by management are suggested.

Rather than being a philosophical treatise about amorphous concepts, *Enterprise Risk Management* is intended as a practical guide, with real life examples and suggestions, to management for the implementation or enhancement of enterprise risk management programmes. Similarly, the board of directors can use this book as a benchmark against which to compare what their organisation has done in this area. As such, it is hoped that the reader will find this a useful contribution to management decision-making in the current challenging economic environment.

Although the framework and general principles would be applicable irrespective of the absolute size and complexity of an organisation, the detailed strategies and controls adopted would inevitably be dependent on the nature, culture and history of the organisation. The definitions of risk, likelihood and impact might also be adjusted to correspond with the particular vision or risk appetite of the organisation.

Ultimately, the responsibility rests with the board of directors to properly execute their fiduciary duties towards all the stakeholders of the organisation. It is hoped that this book provides some of the tools to facilitate those requirements.

Chapter 2

Enterprise Risk Management

Introduction

Corporate governance in general, and its perceived failures in particular, have received a significant amount of political and media coverage as a direct result of the current economic turmoil and banking crises. By extension, enterprise risk management, which is closely related to, and in fact forms an integral part of, the broader principles of corporate governance, has also been subjected to enhanced scrutiny. Thus, in this chapter we will seek first to define and then briefly examine certain aspects of corporate governance before moving on to discussing enterprise risk management itself.

Corporate Governance

At its most basic level, corporate governance is mainly about how, and for what reason, an organisation is being run by its managers. For the purposes of this book, we might therefore define, slightly more formally, the concept as follows:

Corporate governance is the combination and interaction of all the structures and responsibilities of the management of an organisation implemented to achieve its objectives.

Such a definition implies that an organisation, through its management, sets objectives in order to provide benefits to, at a minimum, its shareholders (if not also its wider stakeholders), and ensures that its internal workings are aligned in order to realise those objectives.

For companies listed on the main markets of the London and Irish stock exchanges, *The UK Corporate Governance Code* (2010) (previously called *The Combined Code on Corporate Governance*) encapsulates the existing principles and guidance in support of this concept. Although these principles are not enforceable rules *per se* (unlike the approach adopted by the United States), these listed companies are, however, required to either comply with them or to explain in their annual reports why they have deviated from the guidance.

Whereas the overall definition and scope of corporate governance would be fairly consistent across the various regulatory jurisdictions, the actual implementation guidance can vary significantly. For example, in the UK and Ireland there is a strong emphasis on the segregation between the roles of the chairman (who is also expected to be an independent director) and that of the managing director. In the United States, on the other hand, the roles are typically combined into a single individual. The continental European models of Germany and France advocate a separate supervisory board, whereas the UK model requires a unitary board with a majority of independent directors. It is most likely that these differences have arisen in response to the unique or historic characteristics prevalent in each jurisdiction.

None of the governance models outlined above has been shown to necessarily perform significantly better than any of the others. This is evident from the fact that the same spectacular corporate governance failures seemingly occurred in all of these jurisdictions. It might, therefore, be concluded that the actual model is of less importance than the quality, competence and independence of the individuals tasked with its administration.[1]

Definition of 'Enterprise Risk Management'

The *Corporate Governance Code* indicates, amongst its other guidance, that "the board should maintain a sound system of internal control...".[2] Further on in the Code, this principle is clarified to include an, at least annual, review of all material controls and risk management systems.

In addition to these broad principles, the *Turnbull Report* (1999)[3] provides more detailed guidance to organisations and directors on

---

[1] "Governance Models", *Accountancy Ireland*, Vol. 41 pp. 43–45 December 2009.
[2] Section C.2 of *The UK Corporate Governance Code* (Financial Reporting Council, June 2010).
[3] Lloyd, Bevan, *Guidance on Internal Control* ("The Turnbull Guidance") (Financial Reporting Council, 1999).

the nature and hallmarks of an effective system of internal control. For example, the Report requires that the internal controls be:

- embedded into the operations of the organisation,
- agile and responsive to emerging risks, and
- able to escalate issues to appropriate levels of management when required.[4]

This book aims to build on the principles outlined in the *Corporate Governance Code* and *The Turnbull Guidance* in order to provide a detailed and practical guide to the actual mechanics and issues involved in implementing such a system of internal control. It is, however, important from the outset to highlight the significant caveat, as outlined in *The Turnbull Guidance*, in respect of any system of internal controls.[5] As a system of internal control will ultimately be dependent on human decision-making capabilities, it cannot provide *complete* assurance that all issues would be successfully addressed. It can, however, if properly implemented, provide a reasonable expectation to the board of directors that issues would be effectively mitigated in a timely manner.

Though 'enterprise risk management' is, strictly speaking, a much broader concept than a system of internal control, in general these terms are used somewhat interchangeably. The main difference, for our purposes, is that while a system of internal control focuses more extensively on controls, enterprise risk management encompasses strategies as well as controls. In the context of this book, **strategies** are those activities that have typically a much broader influence on the organisation, commandeer more resources, extend well beyond the finance department to harness the output from multiple functions and undertakings and are, therefore, generally considerably harder to monitor than controls.

Thus, based on the above, we might define **enterprise risk management** as follows:

Enterprise risk management is the combination of all the structures and activities designed to identify and mitigate risk throughout the organisation.

---

[4] Paragraph 22 of *The Turnbull Guidance*.
[5] Paragraph 23 of *The Turnbull Guidance*.

The Goal of Enterprise Risk Management

The ultimate aim or goal of enterprise risk management is to provide accurate information to the correct individuals, typically the board of directors and senior management, in a timely manner so as to allow them to take the appropriate actions. Enterprise risk management provides a consistent mechanism for documentation, analysis and communication of the identified risks, along with their associated mitigation actions, throughout all levels of management within an organisation.

This description of enterprise risk management has three distinct elements to it:

1. accuracy (and completeness) of information;
2. timely and consistent delivery of information; and
3. appropriate actions flowing from such information.

For the purposes of the analysis presented in this book, enterprise risk management is primarily concerned with the first two elements, and we will discuss in further detail the various techniques for gathering information as well as the nature and format of the resultant reporting. The third element, actions flowing from such information, moves more into the realm of corporate governance. Enterprise risk management can, of course, provide recommendations and suggestions to appropriately respond to the information being gathered, but ultimately the responsibility for the actions taken rests with an organisation's board of directors.

The Scope of Enterprise Risk Management

Thus, the remit of corporate governance is generally wider than that of enterprise risk management on its own. Corporate governance is, for example, concerned with issues such as the structure and make-up of the board of directors and the interaction with shareholders in order to try to improve on the management decisions being made. Enterprise risk management, on the other hand, presents only a constituent, albeit a major one, of the overall governance of an organisation. It can be seen as the fundamental part of the engine that generates the information on which the governance decisions ought to be made.

8   *Enterprise Risk Management*

Unlisted companies might very well determine not to adopt the full rigour of all the corporate governance principles, whilst at the same time still seek the benefits of implementing an enterprise risk management programme commensurate with the guidance contained in the *Combined Code*. Their management structures, whether made up of, say, a majority of independent directors or not, would be as dependent as listed entities on accurate and timely information in order to take the appropriate actions.

Also, whereas the principles of corporate governance vary across jurisdictions, the guidance for enterprise risk management remains fairly consistent irrespective of the particular regulatory regime.

The pyramid shown below in **Figure 2.1** is an illustration of the relative scope of each of the above mentioned concepts within an organisation. Corporate governance covers the entire organisation and all of its activities. **Enterprise risk management is more narrowly concerned with only those strategies and controls designed to identify and mitigate risk.** The system of internal control focuses primarily on controls, rather than also on the broader

Figure 2.1:   The Relative Scope of Enterprise Risk Management

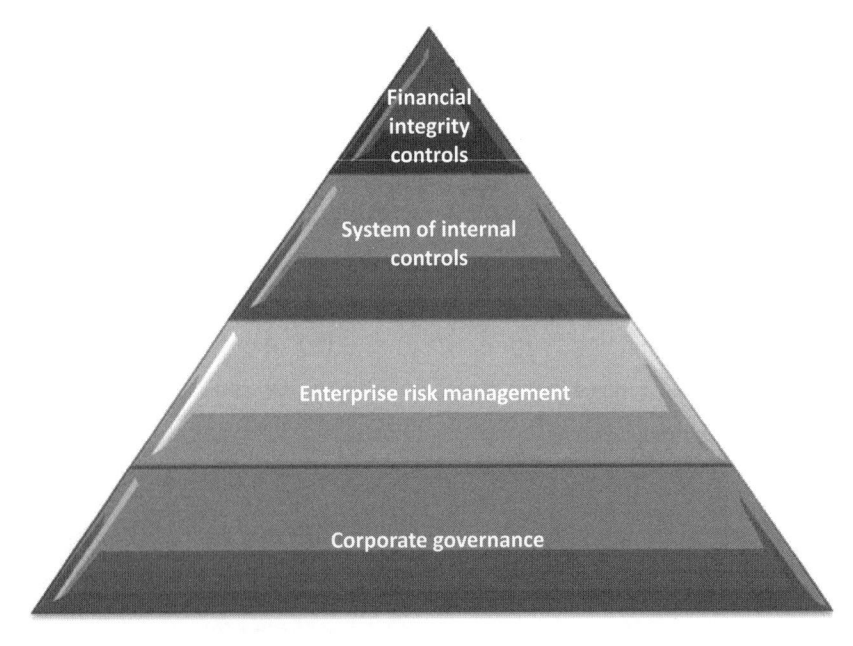

strategies relevant for enterprise risk management. And, finally, the financial integrity controls are focused exclusively on those controls designed to ensure that financial information is accurately recorded and presented.

By way of comparison, it is interesting to note that, for example, the Sarbanes–Oxley legislation applicable to companies listed on the United States exchanges is mainly concerned with the internal controls over financial reporting (or financial integrity controls per our nomenclature), rather than the broader concepts of enterprise risk management.

Conclusion

This chapter has discussed how enterprise risk management is derived from and forms an integral part of the overall corporate governance model of an organisation. In the next chapter we will define some of the specific terminology that will be used in discussing the enterprise risk management programme in the rest of this book.

Chapter 3

What is Risk?

Introduction

In the previous chapter we discussed the origins of enterprise risk management and how it is derived from the broader concept of corporate governance. This chapter sets out to introduce and provide a brief overview of some of the terminology used throughout the enterprise risk management programme. These terms and concepts will then be explored in further detail as part of the subsequent chapters.

Definition of Risk

The key to the proper implementation of an enterprise risk management programme is a detailed understanding of what is meant by the term 'risk'. A somewhat overused and under-appreciated term, 'risk' essentially refers to the fact that future outcomes are of an uncertain nature.

Eventual outcomes are uncertain because, at the outset of any endeavour, there are innumerable factors that may have a bearing on the eventual success or failure of the undertaking.

A further complication is that the exact starting position is not necessarily any more determinable. For example, consider the risk around the acquisition of an existing business. Not only are the forces affecting the future profitability of that business unclear, the assessment of its current position is also highly dependent on the quality of the due diligence undertaken. In that sense, the accuracy of any extrapolation of financial results into the future by the acquirer will be dependent on the robustness of the current financial information.

It is important that management and the board of directors appreciate these inherent limitations of currently available information from the outset. A first step in addressing or mitigating these limitations is to closely define exactly what is meant by 'risk'. For the purposes of this book, we shall use the following approximation:

Risk is the chance that the ultimate result is different from what was expected at the outset.

From the business acquisition example above, one of the risks would therefore be that the purchase price was too high – the cash flow forecast used to support the valuation may turn out to have been too optimistic.

Likelihood and Impact

The basic definition of risk, as outlined above, refers to 'chance' as the value judgement of uncertainty. 'Chance' can then usefully be analysed into its two constituent parts of 'likelihood' and 'impact'. Each of these terms can be expressed in value terms to provide a sense of the quantum of the associated uncertainty.

We will use the impact and likelihood of risk items throughout the rest of this book as key drivers in the risk management process.

Likelihood

It is important for an organisation to define and consistently apply what is understood by it to be the 'likelihood' of risk. Likelihood of a particular risk occurring is typically expressed in percentage term ranges – such that 100% is an absolute certainty and 0% an impossibility. In a risk management framework, 'likelihood' would invariably fall somewhere between these two extremes. Various statistical models have been developed that attempt to precisely calculate the likelihood of any event happening. Of course, such models are prone to the exact same uncertainties that they are trying to quantify. They also typically rely on the principle of *ceteris paribus* – that 'all other factors remain the same'. Recent events at financial institutions have, however, strongly suggested that such models may be overly complex and not necessarily any better as predicative tools.

It is therefore probably sufficient to determine the broader range, rather than the exact percentage point. For example:

- Less than 25% – Low likelihood
- Between 25% and 75% – Medium likelihood
- Greater than 75% – High likelihood.

An alternative classification of the likelihood that a risk will transpire could be based on the timing of events:

- Within the next three months – High likelihood
- Between three months and one year – Medium likelihood
- Beyond one year – Low likelihood.

In using the above classification, insight may be gained into the time horizon of risks. It can act as an early warning system, allowing management to focus on immediate risks rather than ones with a high percentage chance of eventually happening, but not within the next fiscal year.

Impact

It is also important for an organisation to determine what is understood as the impact of a risk. Impact refers to the cost or loss that an organisation will suffer in the event of the risk occurring. Impact, therefore, is typically expressed in monetary values. Organisations often use percentages of their expected profits or equity as the benchmarks for these monetary values. For example:

- Less than 1% of budgeted profit before tax – Low impact
- Between 1% and 5% of budgeted profit before tax – Medium impact
- Greater than 5% of budgeted profit before tax – High impact.

'Upside' Risk

Of course, it might transpire that the ultimate outcome exceeded the original expectations. For example, the return on the investment turned out higher than anticipated or the break-even point was achieved earlier than that predicted by the financial modelling. Typically, though, management are more concerned if a project does not achieve its goals than whether it overachieved. Any uplift will, therefore, be seen as a bonus rather than as a risk. Similarly, this book will primarily focus on 'downside' risk, where the results are different in a negative (rather than positive) way.

'Upside' risk is not to be confused with the opportunity costs inherent in any strategy or control. For the purposes of this book, opportunity costs arise when inefficient mitigation strategies and controls are adopted by an organisation. For example, the organisation might implement a control stating that all expenses to be reimbursed have to be approved by the managing director in advance. This might result in a highly effective control that removes the chance that employees incur inappropriate costs on behalf of the organisation. However, it is also highly inefficient, as it would require the managing director to spend an unacceptable amount of time scrutinising minor or routine expenses. It is one of the main challenges of an enterprise risk management programme to achieve the proper balance between the potentially opposing forces of effectiveness and efficiency.

Categories of Risk

Another aspect that should be clearly defined is the specific category of a risk item into which the risk falls. Assuming that only relevant risks are captured, then those identified risks vary not only by their likelihood and impact but also by their **nature**, i.e., the extent to which they can be managed and controlled. We might therefore categorise risk as follows:

- by response type; and
- by risk appetite.

Risk Categorised by Response Type

The nature and extent of the possible responses from management might result in a useful classification of the associated risks. The following stratification is an example of such a classification:

- external risks;
- internal risks; and
- hybrid risks.

External risks are those risks that fall completely or mostly outside of management's control. These would typically be risks around such areas as the global or domestic economy, interest rates and legislative changes. Another way would be to view these risks as those that impact on the macro-socioeconomic environment in which the organisation operates. Although management would normally be unable to affect the 'likelihood' of these events occurring, they may be able to adopt some strategies and controls that would limit the 'impact' of perceived adverse changes. For example, where an economic downturn is forecast, management may reduce the ensuing pressure on margins by pre-emptively introducing a cost-cutting programme.

Internal risks are those that fall completely or mostly within management's control. These tend to be risks around financial integrity/reporting, fraud, business continuity and product warranty. The strategies and controls adopted by management would be able to affect both the 'likelihood' and 'impact' of such risks. For example, the extent and chance of losses arising from the misappropriation of assets can both be reduced by increasing, say, inventory counts, reducing cash balances on hand and increasing physical security around the warehouses.

Hybrid risks exist in the area between external and internal risks. Whereas management would not be able to fully control such risks, they may be able to influence them. In that sense, the strategies and controls management adopted may be able to affect the 'likelihood' of these risks occurring, rather than the actual 'impact'. For example, shareholder disagreement about the strategic direction of the organisation could invariably have a serious impact, but the likelihood of that happening can be reduced by an independent chairman interacting with the various shareholder groupings, developing a clear vision and co-opting representatives from those groupings as non-executive directors.

This type of classification may be useful to ensure that the responses from management are appropriate and that resources are not wasted trying to affect, e.g. the 'likelihood' of external risks.

Risk Categorised by Risk Appetite

An alternative classification approach would be to stratify the risks according to the risk appetite of the organisation. This speaks to the very heart of the organisation's strategy for creating shareholder returns – the willingness of management to venture the equity of the organisation in the pursuit of profits. The following stratification by risk appetite is an example:

- unavoidable risks;
- avoidable risks; and
- future risks.

Unavoidable risks are those risks that arise from simply being in business in a specific jurisdiction. Although these risks may either fall within or outside of their control, management do not have an option on whether to engage these risks or not. For example, risks around compliance with industry-specific regulations and disaster recovery. Typically, the majority of the identified relevant risks would fall into this category.

Avoidable risks, on the other hand, are those risks that management have already chosen to take on. For example, risks around foreign currency movements and divergent business practices normally only arise when management have determined to trade with or operate in a foreign jurisdiction. To that extent, such risks are optional and reflect on the risk appetite of management. Of course, these risks may have arisen from the strategies (e.g. geographical diversification) that management adopted in response to another risk (such as a domestic recession). Avoidable risks are, therefore, relatively small in number, though they may have potentially significant impact on the organisation. Again such risks may fall either within or outside of the control of management.

Future risks are those risks that do not currently affect the organisation, but which might eventually become relevant, depending on the course of action management decide to embark upon. Assessment of future risks are therefore somewhat similar to a Strengths, Weaknesses, Opportunities and Threats ('SWOT') analysis, but focussing mainly on the 'weaknesses' and 'threats' aspects. For example, before proceeding with an acquisition, management would review whether the incremental risks inherited from the target organisation are still in line with their original risk appetite.

Emerging Risks

Risks are never static and continuously develop and mutate over time. Just as the strategies and controls adopted by management are adapted and revised, so risks also evolve periodically as more information is gathered and initial assumptions are verified. Even eternal risks, such as those around safeguarding of assets, can be more precisely defined as experience is gained and the results from the initial responses to this risk are assessed.

To the extent that risk exists where there is uncertainty of outcome, some risks may, therefore, eventually disappear when that uncertainty has been removed. For example, risk of industrial action following changes to work practices may, in time, become either negligible or in fact crystallise (which might generate various other risks).

Interaction between Risks

We briefly alluded to the fact that individual risks rarely exist in a complete vacuum. Some risks may, in fact, be the direct result of a response to other risks. This raises the possibility of unintended consequences – where management are focused exclusively on a small number of risks without necessarily considering what affect their actions will have on other risks. For example, managing the risk around funding working capital through relentless focusing on delaying payments to creditors may ultimately raise the new risk of sourcing raw materials from suppliers.

Similarly, some risks may result in opportunities in other areas. For example, relative currency strength may be a significant risk to a local distributor where customers can cross a border to purchase goods priced in a relatively weaker currency. On the other hand, that same currency strength may also result in investment or acquisition opportunities for the organisation in that weaker currency jurisdiction. In that sense, some risks can almost be seen as natural hedges against other risks.

Conclusion

In this chapter, we defined what is meant by the concept of 'risk' and briefly introduced some of the other concepts related to this area. In the next chapter we will discuss the building blocks that underpin any risk management programme.

Chapter 4

Required Control Infrastructure

Introduction

This chapter sets out to explore the control infrastructure needed to serve as a basic foundation to the implementation of any enterprise risk management programme. In any organisation there are base-level documents that represent the core of the overall control environment. Examples of such control 'infrastructure' would include:

- a corporate vision statement;
- a code of conduct;
- a fraud policy;
- reporting mechanisms;
- organisational charts; and
- an authorisation matrix.

Although an organisation could choose not to implement all of these building blocks at once, they do tend to work best in conjunction with each other.

Corporate Vision Statement

A corporate vision statement is typically written in broad, inspiring language and encapsulates the high-level strategic goals of the organisation. For example:

> **EXAMPLE: A VISION STATEMENT**
>
> To create a world-class organisation, being either number one or two in every market segment, through leading-edge innovation and global best practices, to drive long-term returns for stakeholders.

The board of directors is normally responsible for creating and developing the vision. As such, it can be seen as the ultimate goal of the organisation from which all other goals, strategies and tactical responses should be distilled. Practices that are in conflict with the vision should, therefore, be discouraged.

Because the vision is set at a high level, it is not expected that it be amended on a frequent basis. Instead, the underlying strategies and tactical responses in support of the vision should be continually re-assessed to ensure that they are still in line with the vision.

From a risk management perspective, useful insight may be gained as to the risk appetite of an organisation from the language used in its vision statement. For example, a newly-appointed managing director, in conjunction with his board, may wish to carve a new strategic direction for the organisation through a change in its vision. This might include an aggressive strategy of diversification into new geographics and businesses. Such a change would then necessarily require an update to the previously identified risks throughout that organisation to reflect the additional risk the organisation wishes to engage in.

Corporate Strategies

From the corporate vision statement, an organisation typically distils corporate strategies to map how the overall vision will be achieved. These strategies are more detailed in nature and explain specific areas of the organisation that will be targeted or harnessed to achieve the vision. The areas normally targeted include areas of specific strength (or weakness) in the organisation. In addition, perennial concerns such as cost-control and cash flow might also be included.

For example, to realise the sample vision as set out above, the organisation might adopt the following strategies:

- acquisition of competitors to achieve market leadership in existing segments;
- annual investment in internal research and development representing a fixed percentage of revenue to secure technological advantage and organic growth;
- strategic stakes in emerging or start-up companies with potentially industry-changing technology;
- focussing on cost reduction through back-office integration; and

- generating free cash flow through shortening the working capital cycle.

The strategies are usually developed by the senior management team and approved by the board of directors. They are generally set for the medium term such that they extend beyond a couple of financial year-ends. However, they might need to be 'tweaked' and perhaps completely changed in order to respond to changes in the environment in which the organisation operates.

Tactical Responses

The corporate strategies are cascaded down to individual managers, who in turn set multiple goals and tasks for their direct reports. These goals typically have detailed measurement criteria and deadlines such that progress towards their achievement can be tracked. For example:

- debtors' days are reduced from 60 days to 55 days by recruiting an additional collections resource;
- the number of patents registered during the financial year is increased from three to five by streamlining internal review processes; and
- increases in administrative overhead costs are contained to less than 3% per year.

Tactical responses are usually relatively short-term and are reviewed on a bi-annual or annual basis.

Performance Management Programmes

The performance management programmes of organisations can vary in their complexity and sophistication. From a risk management perspective, such programmes are particularly useful to ensure that individual goals align with corporate strategies and ultimately the corporate vision.

Through periodic review of the performance of each employee against his set goals, timely corrective action can then be taken where needed. In this way, the programme not only translates the high-level vision into individual, measurable tasks, but also prevents rogue individual actions that conflict with the corporate vision.

Codes of Conduct

Explaining the organisation's attitude towards various day-to-day topics and issues, a code of conduct is typically a more detailed document than the corporate vision.

An organisation's code of conduct is particularly important for setting and espousing the appropriate 'tone at the top'. The nature of the behaviour that is condoned or condemned in the code will similarly permeate the culture of the entire organisation. It is therefore critically important that the code of conduct is clear and unambiguous with regard to behaviour that is not tolerated by the organisation.

An organisation may attach such importance to its code of conduct that it publishes it to an external audience, e.g. via its Website. The organisation might then encourage its suppliers, customers and other stakeholders to report instances where the organisation does not live up to what is set out in its code of conduct.

The level of detail contained in an organisation's code of conduct is a matter for the board of directors to determine. Organisations may opt for either a principles-based or rules-based approach.

Principles-based Codes of Conduct

As the name suggests, a principles-based code tries to avoid detailed or prescriptive requirements by only capturing and listing out the values of the organisation. A principles-based approach normally works well where the organisation is either small, fairly homogenous in its activities or operates in jurisdictions that are culturally similar. Such organisations may determine that it is sufficient to allow a high measure of individual interpretation of what constitutes acceptable behaviour, because it is unlikely to ever stray beyond the acceptable norms. Organisations may find that the 'softer tone' of the principles-based approach, in contrast to the more dictatorial rules-based approach (discussed below), fits better with their own internal culture.

Also, organisations that have adopted a business model where the corporate (or centralised) functions are limited and the decision-making authority is extensively devolved to lower levels, may find that a principles-based approach is consistent with the philosophy that all employees know and understand what appropriate behaviours are.

Principles-based codes of conduct are typically much shorter in length and intentionally make use of vague language and amorphous concepts to avoid setting specific rules and requirements. For example, the entire code may be captured in a couple of bullet points, as below:

> **EXAMPLE: CODE OF CONDUCT (PRINCIPLES-BASED)**
>
> All employees are expected to live not only the letter, but also the spirit of these principles:
>
> - Always act with integrity in all your dealings.
> - Avoid embarrassing the organisation or fellow employees.
> - Avoid compromising or conflicting interests with the organisation.
> - Treat everyone with respect.
> - Focus on enhancing the workplace environment for everyone.

Because with principles-based codes of conduct there is an increased possibility that employees may in fact misinterpret such codes, they are typically augmented with either fairly detailed 'Frequently Asked Questions' or extensive training programmes and workshops to help explain the practical implementation of the principles.

Rules-based Codes of Conduct

A rules-based approach, on the other hand, can be required where the organisation is either large, dispersed or is rapidly expanding into new businesses or jurisdictions. The board of directors may then determine that in order to ensure a smooth integration and alignment of the culture of, for example, an acquired business, a more explicit approach is needed. Similarly, where the organisation operates in a highly regulated or sensitive industry (such as financial services and pharmaceuticals) this approach may also be applicable.

At a minimum, a rules-based code of conduct would generally include the following topics or areas:

- enforceability and application;
- overall values or best practice behaviours;

- prohibited activities, such as:
  - harassment or discrimination;
  - bribery and corruption;
  - disclosure of confidential information; and
  - conflicts of interest.
- encouraged activities, such as:
  - sustainability;
  - health and safety; and
  - interaction with other stakeholders.

Every organisation should of course determine the level of prescription associated with each of these areas so as to be commensurate with its culture and ethos. The following is an extract from an example of what such a rules-based code of conduct might look like:

> ### Example: Extract From Code of Conduct (Rules-based)
>
> *Applicability*
> The Code is applicable to all employees, permanent, part-time, contractors or consultants across all divisions and all of their activities in respect of the organisation.
>
> *Compliance and breaches*
> The ultimate responsibility for ensuring compliance with the Code rests with the Board of Directors. The Board has delegated the implementation of and compliance with the Code to the management teams of each of the divisions.
>
> Contravention of the letter or spirit of the Code is a serious matter. Disciplinary procedures, subject to legal restrictions, will be taken against employees that breach the Code.
>
> Employees are encouraged to report any actual or perceived breaches of the Code through the established channels. There will be no retaliation against employees that make reports in good faith.
>
> *Bribery and corruption*
> No employee will offer or accept cash or other benefits to unlawfully secure or influence a business transaction. The management

teams of each division continue to monitor applicable law in their jurisdiction to ensure consistent compliance.

Conflicts of interest
Employees should avoid situations whereby their personal interests conflict, or are perceived to be in conflict, with those of the organisation.

Employees should obtain the approval of their direct line manager prior to engaging in such activities or as soon as they become aware of such a conflict.

Confidential information
Employees may not disclose or share confidential information outside of the organisation unless specifically authorised in writing by their managing director to do so. Employees should also ensure that the disclosure of any non-confidential information does not negatively impact on the reputation of the organisation.

Donations to politicians or political parties
The organisation does not allow the making of donations or any other payments to any political official or organisation in any jurisdiction that it operates in, unless mandated by law.

Harassment and discrimination
The organisation does not allow harassment or unlawful discrimination against any employee. The management teams of each division continue to monitor applicable law in their jurisdiction to ensure consistent compliance.
...

Although the language of such a code of conduct is specifically designed to provide clarity in respect of what constitutes acceptable behaviour, it may be perceived as overly prescriptive and overbearing by employees.

Ultimately, the tone, approach and detail of the code of conduct should be informed by the culture already prevalent in the organisation and the extent to which the board of directors wishes to encourage or moderate that culture. The code of conduct should be a 'living document' that employees and other stakeholders find a useful and informative guide against which to benchmark their behaviour.

Beyond Codes of Conduct

Some organisations have started to think beyond just the documentation of their code of conduct and are increasing their focus on ways to make the code of conduct 'come alive' for their employees, so that the values outlined therein become embedded in their everyday business interactions. Some of the techniques that such organisations use to achieve this include:

- Orientation and training
- Periodic certification of compliance
- Newsletters
- Feedback channels
- Dedicated ethics programmes
- Frequently Asked Questions (of FAQs)

Frequently asked questions, as indicated above, can be particularly helpful in supporting a high-level principles-based code of conduct. Everyday scenarios that have or are likely to present themselves to employees are considered with reference to the underlying code of conduct. This is a way to clarify the rules of the code of conduct in a non-confrontational manner. Organisations should, however, take care to ensure consistency across the various answers to the FAQs. Whereas a single code of conduct will necessarily be consistent, an increase in literature around the code of conduct will raise the possibility of ambiguities, contradictions and 'loop holes'.

Training courses can also be developed to explain the rationale for the code of conduct in general and each of its specific requirements in particular. Such training can be made mandatory for any new recruits as part of their induction and orientation into the culture of the organisation.

Some organisations insist on periodic (typically annual) **certification** whereby employees are required to sign off that they understand and follow the requirements of the code of conduct. Such certification plans may be coupled with training programmes to leverage their effectiveness.

It has also been found that regular **communication from senior executives** to all employees throughout the organisation around ethics and the code of conduct may help cascade the correct 'tone at the top'. The chief executive, for example, may include a couple of paragraphs on a pertinent aspect of the code of conduct in his quarterly newsletter to staff. He may also wish to include an outline of the organisation's responses to changes in the environment in which it operates and how these actions align with the code of conduct.

Feedback channels are important ways for organisations to identify emerging issues that employees are faced with. These channels are not necessarily hotlines to report breaches, but are rather mechanisms whereby staff can seek clarification as to what appropriate behaviour should be in a specific, to-date unforeseen, circumstance. This helps to ensure that an organisation's code of conduct remains up-to-date and relevant for its employees.

Because the 'tone at the top' is of such critical importance, organisations may decide to invest in **dedicated ethics programmes** for its senior executives. Such organisations are conscious that senior executives act as role models to other employees and that their behaviours and actions eventually permeate throughout the organisation. The ethics programmes are generally hosted by external specialists who can provide the necessary insights into current best practices or suggest alternative approaches and considerations in dealing with ethical dilemmas. In this way, an organisation can remain open to challenging existing practices and implementing new ideas when required.

Fraud Policy

Organisations typically pay particular attention to the issue of fraud. We will return to the various issues associated with an organisation's response to the risk of fraud in **Chapter 9**. At this stage, it is sufficient to outline certain considerations around the establishment of a fraud policy.

Some organisations include a section on fraud within their general code of conduct, while others create a stand-alone document on fraud. A possible reason for this latter approach is that an organisation may want to be particularly explicit with regard to fraud and that the wording used in this regard may not necessarily be consistent with a principles-based, externally available code of conduct that is published on the organisations' external website.

Either way, it is important to precisely define what the organisation regards as fraud. Given that there may be legal requirements around the reporting of suspected frauds to regulatory authorities, organisations may determine to engage with internal or external legal counsel in drafting their fraud policies.

The fraud policy normally includes a clear and unambiguous statement that fraud is not tolerated by the organisation and will be pursued in accordance with the policy and the applicable legal requirements.

It may also outline how a suspected fraud should be reported and what the general process is in this regard. It is important that the fraud policy explicitly clarifies that no retaliation would be taken against bona fide reports of suspected breaches.

The organisation should ensure that employees are fully aware of the fraud policy and may therefore decide to introduce training programmes to that effect. This is particularly the case where the organisation operates in jurisdictions where instances of fraud may be more endemic or perceived to be acceptable.

An example of a stand-alone fraud policy is shown below:

EXAMPLE: FRAUD POLICY

Definition
Fraud may involve any or all of the following activities:

- the intentional misrepresentation of the financial position or results of any business within the organisation;
- the theft of assets such as inventory, equipment or cash;
- the falsification of records or authorisations to extract economic value from the organisation; and
- corruption or bribery.

Reporting
The organisation does not tolerate fraud at any level. It is the policy of the organisation, subject to legal restrictions, to dismiss and prosecute any employee involved with fraud.

Employees are expected to report detected or suspected fraud to their direct line managers or by using the whistleblower hotline. There will be no retaliation against employees that make reports in good faith.

Standard process
All suspected cases of fraud are brought to the immediate attention of the Audit Committee of the Board of Directors, who then

nominate an investigation team with the appropriate skills and experience. Where necessary, the appropriate external regulatory authorities are also informed.

The team prepares a report to the Audit Committee outlining the scope and findings of its investigation as well as any recommendations. The Audit Committee determines the appropriate remedial action (and sanctions if applicable).

Alternate Processes

Organisations may adopt various different processes for responding to an instance of suspected fraud depending again, to some degree, on the culture within the individual organisation. For example, the following categories or terms can be used for such investigations:

- ad hoc corporate investigation team;
- corporate internal audit;
- outside specialists; or
- divisional management.

Ad hoc corporate investigation team An ad hoc team may be sufficient where the instances of suspected fraud are normally few or relate to a new jurisdiction or business recently invested in. In such cases, the audit committee may wish to be closely involved to determine whether this is an indication of a more pervasive threat requiring a general revision to strategies and controls. The benefit of such a specialised team is that they typically involve senior personnel with extensive experience, which would likely result in thorough investigations. On the other hand, these senior personnel may be constrained in the time that they can devote to any investigation, resulting in a dragged-out process.

Internal audit If such a department exists within the organisation, internal audit is typically well-placed to launch an independent investigation. Their training and knowledge of the detailed procedures and controls of the organisation would allow them to effectively pin-point where the breakdown occurred and propose appropriate remediation. They are also more familiar with the organisational culture than, say, outside specialists, so their investigations may be more in-depth and revealing.

Outside specialists Where the suspected fraud is complex or particularly sensitive (for example, involving senior executives) outside specialists may be necessary. Their varied experience would allow them a totally independent perspective of how and why the breakdown occurred. Care should be taken, however, that their proposed remediation is consistent with the culture of the organisation and therefore workable in practice.

Senior management Senior management of the division or department where the suspected fraud took place may, in certain circumstances, be appropriate to quickly investigate and conclude on it. Care should however be taken that the scope of such an investigation is transparent and appropriate, and that it is done on an independent basis. The team can be made up of senior management from other divisions or departments to ensure an 'at-arm's length' approach.

Of course, any investigation team can include members from each of the categories mentioned above to enhance the overall effectiveness of the team.

On the other hand, organisations may also decide that the *type* of fraud will determine the actual investigation process to be followed. For example, suspected fraud in respect of employee expense claims can perhaps be resolved within the relevant division or department itself, rather than involving the audit committee directly. Typically then, the audit committee will only receive a status update of the number of frauds, amounts involved and remedial actions adopted by each division.

Where the financial results of a division or department have been manipulated, a team from the corporate head office or senior management outside of that department may be more appropriate to conduct the investigation.

Ultimately, it is important that whatever process for responding to suspected fraud is chosen, it is seen to have validity. The board of directors must satisfy themselves that the scope of the investigation is sufficient, that due process has been followed, that the conclusions reached are fair and that the recommendations for remediation, if implemented, are likely to be effective to avoid similar issues in the future.

Reporting Mechanisms

Policies such as the code of conduct are useful to document and explain expected behaviour. Their effectiveness is, however, largely dependent on the quality of the compliance monitoring associated with them.

Organisations are to a large extent reliant on either internal or external sources to bring non-compliance to their attention. There are a number of ways in which an organisation can "establish channels of communication for individuals to report suspected breaches of laws or regulations or other improprieties" as indicated by the Turnbull Guidance.[6] For example, individuals may

- report to direct line manager,
- report to an independent department,
- use a confidential helpline, or
- use anonymous suggestion boxes.

Organisations may decide to adopt a number of these channels in conjunction with each other so as to ensure as much coverage as possible.

Reporting to Direct Line Manager

The direct line manager route follows the established chart of the organisation. While, typically, it would minimise spurious allegations, it could also possibly reduce the number of legitimate concerns being raised. It may work well in smaller organisations or where there is an open culture or well-established interaction between managers and subordinates. Where, of course, the direct manager is suspected of being involved in the wrongdoing, the process should allow for the issue to be raised at the next level up – the manager's manager – in the reporting chain.

Depending on the nature and complexity of the allegations raised, line managers may not necessarily have the requisite skills to adequately deal with it or appreciate the need for immediate escalation. Organisations that solely rely on this process should, therefore, strongly consider designing appropriate training for all their line managers in how to deal with allegations of impropriety.

Reporting to an Independent Department

Organisations may also determine that in order to encourage employees to raise all concerns, any such reports are to be made to an independent department. These would typically either be the human resources, internal audit, risk management or legal departments.

---

[6] Appendix to *The Turnbull Guidance*.

These departments can have specific skills allowing them to gather the appropriate information and communicate it to the relevant investigation team.

On the other hand, in larger organisations, employees may be reluctant to raise their concerns with strangers, especially if the process around the ensuing investigation is not widely known or understood.

Confidential Helpline

Larger organisations also typically establish a confidential helpline or whistleblower hotline. Such a system is normally maintained by an outside provider and can include sophisticated case management tools. These tools allow for progress on investigations to be tracked and analysed for trends as well as generating reports for the audit committee or senior executives. A specific department or individual, normally at the corporate head office, is nominated to receive and allocate (in accordance with the pre-determined investigative process) the initial allegation.

Critically, a hotline also allows anonymous two-way communication in the sense that the investigation team can request additional information and provide updates on the investigation through such systems. It is important for the validity of the process that whistleblowers understand that breaches are taken seriously and that the related investigation is being actively progressed.

Typically, such a helpline is also externally accessible, and third parties, such as customers, suppliers and other stakeholders, may be similarly inclined to report suspected breaches. This is especially the case where an organisation publishes its code of conduct on its external Website along with the telephone number of the hotline.

Recent research[7] has, however, indicated that these hotlines are currently underutilised in Ireland.

An organisation may consider establishing a system whereby rogue comments are filtered prior to escalation to an investigation team. Resources can then be focused on allegations with at least prima facie substance. It may also help to minimise spurious allegations against innocent employees.

---

[7] PricewaterhouseCoopers, *Economic crime in a downturn: The Global Economic Crime Survey* (November 2009) (www.pwc.com/ie/en/economic-crime-survey-2009/index.jhtml)

Suggestion Boxes

The use of suggestion boxes is another way in which senior management can be alerted anonymously to suspected improprieties. This can be especially useful in an organisation where a confidential helpline has not been set up.

These secured post boxes are typically located in easily accessible locations and frequently reviewed by a designated department or individual. Employees are normally also encouraged to submit suggestions or improvements beyond only allegations of breaches.

A significant drawback of this system is, however, the one-way nature of its communication. An investigation team may require additional information or clarification, which would not be available through this channel. Furthermore, employees may become discouraged if they get a sense that nothing has happened to address their concerns, not necessarily appreciating how long many investigations can take.

Organisational Charts

An organisation can normally document its reporting structure by means of an organisational chart. This is relevant from a risk management perspective because it clarifies who the line manager is of each employee and, in turn, to whom that manager reports. Ultimately, all reporting lines feed into the board of directors as the primary authority.

An organisational chart may also assist in determining whether certain employees are performing duties that are potentially conflicted. For example, an employee who is tasked with creating new vendor accounts (and reports to the purchasing manager) should typically not also be responsible for reconciling creditor statements or making payments (reporting to the finance manager). (We will return to the topic of segregation of duties as part of the fraud risk assessment section of **Chapter 9**.)

An organisation may wish to distinguish between direct reporting (normally shown as a solid line on organisational charts) and indirect reporting (normally shown as a dotted line). Certain employees may report to their line manager on a day-to-day basis, but also receive instruction from other parties in the organisation. For example, an internal auditor may formally report directly to the audit committee, but for normal everyday interaction report to the finance director. Organisations should take care that every employee understands clearly who he or she reports to and takes instruction from. Confusion in this respect may increase the potential for the circumvention of internal control.

An example of an organisational chart is shown in **Figure 4.1**:

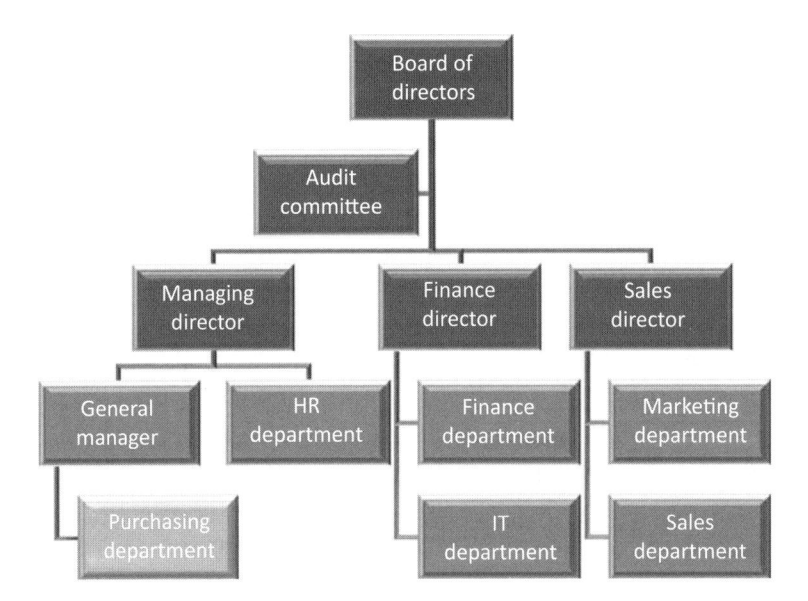

Figure 4.1: An Organisational Chart

```
                    Board of
                   directors
                       |
                     Audit
                   committee
        _____|_____
       |                   |                   |
   Managing            Finance              Sales
   director            director            director
    ___|___         _____|_____         ____|____
   |       |       |             |       |         |
General   HR     Finance        IT    Marketing  Sales
manager  dept.   dept.         dept.  dept.      dept.
   |
Purchasing
department
```

Group or Company Policies

Whereas a code of conduct provides broad direction on the values and behaviour that an organisation expects, group or company policies are the detailed manuals (sometimes called **employee handbooks**) with step-by-step instructions on everyday non-financial business activities and interactions.

The detailed contents of such a policy manual will depend to a large degree on the nature of the organisation. Organisations may wish to be prescriptive on matters ranging from, say, dress code to sick leave, where they believe that that would assist in creating or enhancing a common or homogenous culture. Alternatively, less prescription may encourage individualism at the expense of uniformity.

It is advisable, therefore, that organisations should take care when documenting their detailed policies to reflect the existing and desired culture.

Organisations should then establish training programmes for their employees in application of these policies as well as mechanisms whereby questions or suggestions can be resolved.

Compliance with these non-financial policies is normally tracked by the direct line managers of the employees or more generally the human resources department.

Accounting Policies

The accounting policies of an organisation specifically deal with its financial reporting requirements and cover such topics as the rates of depreciation of various fixed asset categories or the method for recognising revenue on different types of sales contracts.

The pertinent accounting policies are typically reflected in the annual financial statements, especially where the applicable accounting regime (be it Irish GAAP or IFRS) allows for alternative approaches. Where the organisation consists of more than one legal entity, it is important for consolidation purposes to ensure that the accounting policies are consistent across the group.

Due to their nature, accounting policies are normally only circulated within the various finance departments across the organisation. Ongoing training (either internally generated or sourced from external specialist providers) in the application of these policies may be required as the underlying accounting regimes are continuously updated.

Organisations typically rely on an internal audit function, either in-house or outsourced, to monitor compliance with its accounting policies. External audits may also reveal errors in the interpretation or application of these policies.

Authorisation Matrix

An organisation is ultimately headed by its board of directors. They may, however, determine that it is both effective and efficient to delegate some of their authority to management at lower levels throughout the organisation. An authority matrix should clearly set out the nature and extent of such delegated authority.

The extent of the delegation is largely predicated by the culture of the organisation, although it is important to note the default position – any authority not delegated by the board of directors remains with them. Therefore, groups with a strong 'federalist' ethos would typically have more extensive delegation to levels below the group managing director. Alternatively, groups with a large, well-developed corporate head office would tend to have less authority delegated to divisional management. For smaller organisations, the delegation of authority would relate to departmental management, instead of divisional management.

Achieving this balance is a key decision for management. Overcentralisation of authority may undermine initiative from the divisions, whereas over-delegation may undermine control and overall strategic focus.

The authority matrix typically places a limit or monetary range on the transactions or decisions that are allowed for each level of the organisation. It is generally an upwards approach in the sense that where a specific investment requires board approval it has been preapproved by the relevant divisional and group management. This is typically done to ensure that lower level management, who will eventually be responsible for the success of the transactions, have bought into its business justification.

An example of an authority matrix is shown below:

EXAMPLE: AUTHORITY MATRIX

Head of the division/head of the department (for smaller organisations)
- Capital expenditure less than €1,000,000 per project
- Impairment of fixed assets less than €100,000
- Press releases concerning the division only

Group managing director/managing director (for smaller organisations)
- Capital expenditure between €1,000,000 and €5,000,000

- Impairment of assets between €100,000 and €1,000,000
- Divesting from a business at a loss less than €100,000
- Press releases with potential implications for the group

Board of directors
- Acquisition of new businesses
- Diversification into foreign jurisdictions
- Capital expenditure in excess of €5,000,000 per project
- Impairment of assets in excess of €1,000,000
- Divesting from a business at a loss greater than €100,000

Terms of Reference

The board of directors may delegate specific areas of its authority to sub committees. This is typically necessary to comply with the Combined Code or where specialist knowledge is required. As is normal with delegation, decisions made by such sub committees would be binding on the board as a whole.

The following sub-committees are commonly used:

- audit committee;
- nomination committee; and
- remuneration committee.

The board of directors may determine that the nature of the activities of the organisation is such that additional specialist committees are warranted. For example:

- tendering committee; and
- business development committee.

Organisations that, for example, engage in public–private partnerships (PPPs) may determine that due to the complexity of those tendering considerations a specialist committee is warranted. Similarly, highly acquisitive organisations may decide that a dedicated business development committee is required to oversee the due diligence and negotiation processes.

In all cases, it is important to precisely document the terms of reference of these committees. This is to ensure that the committees are properly mandated and that there is no overlap or gaps in what has been delegated to them. The chairman of the board of directors is usually responsible for the review of the appropriateness of the delegated authorities by virtue of his duty to ensure the smooth and proper functioning of the board.

Terms of reference of the committees normally cover the following captions:

- membership,
- duties,
- meetings, and
- other administrative matters.

Membership refers to whether executive directors or only non-executive directors are participants. It also specifies the nature of any specialist knowledge or experience required from the participants.

Duties outline in detail the delegated areas of responsibility. For example, the audit committee is generally responsible for the integrity of the annual financial statements, the review of the risk management system and the interaction with the external auditors. The nomination committee is typically responsible for the succession planning at board level and interviewing potential new directors. The remuneration committee, on the other hand, is responsible for reviewing the compensation paid to executive directors and other senior managers.

Meetings refer not only to the number of meetings held, but also to what would constitute a quorum for decision-making.

Other administrative matters refer, for example, to the access of members to external specialists and performance appraisal mechanisms for the committee.

Conclusion

In this chapter we discussed the various building blocks that should underpin any enterprise risk management programme. In the next chapter we will review the organisational structures specifically related to the implementation of such a risk management programme.

Chapter 5

Organisational Structures of Risk Management

Introduction

In the preceding chapter, we reviewed the building blocks that provide the base for a system of internal control. In this chapter we will consider the specific organisational structures required for implementing an enterprise risk management programme.

Executive Sponsorship

For some organisations, implementing a risk management process may require significant new resources, time and changes in established procedures or structures. It is therefore critically important that such an initiative receives the appropriate sponsorship from senior executives.

The managing director may, for example, as part of his communication to staff in the company newsletter introduce the idea and rationale for its implementation. He may explain the need for the process and the expected benefits that may be realised from it. In this manner, local management would be alerted to the process and what would be required or expected from them.

In particular, senior executives should set the appropriate 'tone at the top' to ensure that local management give due regard to the goals of the process and engage in a meaningful and sincere way.

Ultimately, the quality of the risk management process will be determined to a large degree by the level of commitment and engagement from the management of each business unit or department. Therefore, the board of directors may determine to nominate a specific executive director as 'owner' of the process, who will track progress and provide advice to whoever is tasked with the actual implementation.

Organisational Structure

Once the executive sponsor has been nominated, an organisation can use a number of different organisational structures or departments for the actual implementation of the risk management process. For example, the following departments may be designated as the implementors and monitors of the risk management process:

- internal audit department;
- legal and compliance department;
- finance department;
- risk management department; or
- decentralised model.

Internal Audit Department

The remit of an internal audit department typically includes verifying compliance with the internal control procedures of the organisation. The focus is normally on financial controls but may, on occasion, extend also to include other business areas, for example, efficiency testing in warehouses.

Internal audit usually has well-developed test plans and procedures. In addition, it would have established channels of communication whereby findings are agreed with local management before being shared and analysed with senior executives and the audit committee.

Internal audit, therefore, has the tools and mechanisms already in place to monitor compliance with established rules and controls.

On the other hand, the background and experience of the internal audit team may not be best-suited to assess and develop the broader strategic risks facing the organisation. They may also be constrained by limits on resources and pre-established commitments in respect of testing financial controls.

Legal and Compliance Department

Organisations of a certain size or complexity may have already established in-house legal departments whose focus is, amongst other matters, to ensure compliance with laws and regulations.

These departments tend to employ only a limited number of specialists (typically with legal backgrounds) and might therefore lack the manpower or resources to embark on an extensive risk management process. Their experience might similarly be limited in respect of verifying compliance and reporting back on recommendations in respect of broader business, strategic and financial risks.

Finance Department

Finance departments typically also have a history of developing policies and procedures to address the processing of financial transactions. They might, therefore, have particular insights into the emergence of risk as translated into the financial results of business units.

The department might, however, be constrained by the availability of resources from expanding their interaction with business units outside of the already established financial reporting channels.

Risk Management Department

This is a dedicated function that is usually based at the corporate head office. It is staffed by employees that generally have strong financial backgrounds, but also some experience of internal controls and processes.

As a result of the closely defined role of the department, its activities could be focused on the implementation and, critically, the maintenance of the risk management process.

The department can also be the nominated recipient of reports made through the anonymous hotline as well as leading or participating in the resulting investigation team. The required set of skills to manage an investigation can be developed and maintained within the department, rather than having the knowledge and experience dissipating once an ad hoc team completes its work and disbands.

The monitoring of compliance can still be outsourced to the in-house internal audit department or to third party providers to avoid duplication with other departments.

Similar to the internal audit department, the risk management department may also have a direct reporting line to the audit committee to ensure independence and avoid undue influence from senior executives.

The size of the risk management department is dependent on the overall complexity and diversity of the organisation, as well as the expected timeframe for the roll-out of the risk management process. Normally, the department would consist of a manager and one or more staff members. The role of the staff would be to perform the detailed interviews or assessments and to prepare the draft versions of the resulting reports. The role of the manager would be to define and allocate the workload to the staff members, review the reports, discuss and agree the results with local management and present the findings to the board of directors.

Where the department has more than one staff member, the assessment process can be run in parallel, such that multiple business units can participate at the same time. The manager of the department should, however, ensure through appropriate oversight and review that the quality and approach of the staff members are consistent across the business units.

Decentralised Model

Depending on the culture of the organisation, the implementation of the risk management process might be delegated to each individual business unit or department. Local management would then be responsible for all aspects of the process and typically only report back to the board of directors (through the corporate head office) via a certification that the process has been completed and updated.

In a sense, most business units already conduct their own internal risk management programmes through strategy meetings, marketing plans and procedure manuals. The overall process tends, however, to be infrequent, informal or too focused on particular risks to the exclusion of a more generalised approach.

Therefore, the consistency of approach in a decentralised model would depend on the quality of instruction from the corporate head office as well as the time and resource commitments from local management.

It is normally expected then that, where an organisation has determined that a formalised risk management process is appropriate, and indeed required, such a process be driven from the corporate head office, rather than relying solely on the local business units to develop their own programmes. For smaller organisations, this would require individual departments or functions to align their risk management processes with one another.

Roll-out of the Process

In **Chapter 6** we will examine in detail the various steps of a risk management process. An organisation may determine that a 'Big Bang' approach is required whereby all the business units are effectively participating at the same time. This may be necessary where the organisation is under time pressure to introduce a risk management process. This approach may also lead, however, to 'teething' issues if the design of the process was not optimal from the outset. Such issues would then have to be addressed through some form of reverse-engineering or possibly even re-starting the process from the beginning.

An alternative is first to launch the process on a pilot basis. A single business unit or department is selected and its risk management process is completed before the programme is rolled out for the rest of the organisation.

The benefits of a pilot scheme are that it allows the process to be adjusted and adapted based on the experience gained from the single location. It might be found that the desk-top planning (being the work performed in advance of the actual field work) is not at all consistent with the realities on the ground. Because of the limited scope of the initial roll-out, any modifications required would be limited in nature and resource allocations. If the process at the pilot location was then so significantly flawed that it would require a re-performance, that business unit could be revisited at the end of the overall process so as not to impose too great a time burden on local management.

An organisation should, therefore, take care when deciding which business unit should act as the pilot location. The following considerations may be appropriate in selecting the pilot location:

- established business model with no significant new product lines or markets;
- stable operating environment with limited recent changes to processes and IT applications;
- experienced local management team that is ideally familiar with the principles of a risk management process;

- low level of unusual or unique risks expected;
- relatively minor operations preferably confined to a single or small number of geographic jurisdictions; and
- homogenous business activities in the context of the overall group.

The actual criteria for determining the appropriate pilot location might of course be different from those outlined above. However, it is important that the pilot is conducted in an established business unit with defined procedures already implemented and where the majority of the management team have been in place for some period of time. The board of directors or senior executives would, therefore, most likely not expect significant new risks to emerge as a result of the risk management process. Instead, the business unit can be used as a benchmark against which to measure the performance of the risk management process itself.

The board of directors and senior executives can also provide feedback on the nature and extent of reporting generated from the process. A further consideration could be the logistical aspects of visiting the pilot location. Ideally, the pilot location would be geographically close or accessible to the corporate head office so that where additional information is required, revisiting that location would not involve significant travelling. For smaller organisations with a limited number of business units, the pilot location might instead be a specific department such as human resources. This would also allow for the pilot location to potentially be visited more frequently, resolving emerging issues, than would normally be expected for the other business units once the process is up and running.

A successful implementation at the pilot location would also enhance the credibility of the overall process, especially where positive feedback from that local management team is received.

Communication

It is important that open communication is maintained throughout the process. Typically, the findings for each business unit are summarised in a report to the board of directors either directly or, more generally, via senior management.

In advance of sharing the report with the board of directors, local management should be satisfied with its content in respect of their business unit. It may be necessary for the report to have to go through various iterations and revisions before it is finalised. Ultimately, where a disagreement with local management cannot be resolved, their responses should be included verbatim in the report. The board of directors can then act as a final arbiter in the resolution of the issue. (We will discuss in **Chapter 10** the potential challenges and barriers applicable to implementing a risk management process.)

The reports to the board of directors would normally be standardised and include the following broad headings:

- Executive summary and overall conclusion
- Outline of approach
- Detailed supporting schedules

Executive Summary

The executive summary should typically be limited to a couple of paragraphs containing the overall risk impression gained from the relevant business unit. It may also indicate a rating of the control environment and highlight significant or immediate areas of risk.

The overall rating can be categorised as follows:

- Strong / good;
- Adequate / fair;
- Ineffective / poor; or
- Start-up / interim.

A **strong** rating would generally be appropriate where the assessment indicates that local management have a thorough understanding and appreciation of the risks facing their business unit and had already implemented well-designed strategies and controls to mitigate them. The recommendations identified would essentially be of a documentary nature or require relatively minor re-design of existing processes and procedures.

An **adequate** rating would generally be appropriate where management also have a broad understanding of risk, but where some additional procedures are required to be introduced or some existing processes to be re-designed. The recommendations would then typically provide additional information in respect of these areas, but would generally extend beyond merely documentary changes.

An **ineffective** rating would be appropriate where management have either completely missed significant risks facing their business units or have not implemented appropriate controls and strategies to address those risks. Therefore, an extensive re-design of the overall control framework of the business unit might be required.

A **start-up** rating is appropriate where the design of proposed strategies can only be assessed in the future. For example, where a new business unit has only recently been created it might still be a helpful roadmap to assist local management in designing controls that are expected to result in appropriate risk mitigating responses. However, the validity of those assumptions can only be tested once the business unit has been trading for a period so as to allow most of the responses to have operated.

The board of directors may, of course, determine that additional rating categories are needed to more closely compare different business units. Sliding scales ranging from 1–5 or even 1–10 can then be used to describe the overall conclusion. However, experience indicates that a standard 'bell curve' dispersion exists, irrespective of the detail of the scaling used. This means that the majority of business units would normally be expected to be rated as "fair", with a much smaller number of business units classified on either side of that mean.

There could also be a potential over-emphasis on the actual rating given to a business unit. The ultimate goals of a risk management process are to identify and mitigate risk. Therefore, the detailed comments and recommendations should be of more importance than the single word conclusion. (We will return to this area as part of **Chapter 10**.)

The rating might be augmented with a short commentary on key areas identified during the risk review. For example, where an 'adequate rating' is deemed to be appropriate, it might be useful to explain, in the Summary, the broader areas for improvement, such as segregation of duties, or specific points of concern, such as incorrect accounting treatments. Care should however be taken that these highlighted areas do not become the only action items to the detriment of the other recommendations.

Outline of Approach

The approach adopted in formulating the report to the board of directors should be extensively described. This is to avoid confusion in respect of the scope or nature of the process. (We will discuss, for example, the various methods of gathering the information in **Chapter 6**.)

It is important to further document the timeframe to which that the assessment relates. This is to indicate that the assessment reflects a specific point in time and would require continuous revision and reassessment over a period of time. Also, any significant subsequent events or emerging risks would clearly fall outside of the scope of the initial assessment.

The names and positions of the members of local management that participated in the assessment should also be listed. This allows the board to determine whether the appropriate managers participated in the process and enables them then to conclude whether the process was robust enough to reveal the significant risks at that particular business unit.

Critically, any limitations to the standard approach should be clearly outlined in the report. For example, whether key management personnel were unavailable during the assessment process, or that no controls were tested beyond assessing their design effectiveness, etc. These limitations may then be addressed during follow-up assessments when deemed necessary.

Detailed Supporting Schedules

We will discuss the various risk registers and maps that can be used to document an assessment in the next chapter. It probably makes sense to include such detail findings as appendices to the main report. Due to time constraints, the board of directors may only be interested in the Executive Summary once they are satisfied that the overall approach adopted in the assessment process is sufficient. Local management, on the other hand, should use the detailed schedules as a checklist to ensure that all issues identified are appropriately addressed.

Recommendations

The department implementing the process may identify certain recommendations in respect of the design of the responses introduced by local management to mitigate the related risks.

These recommendations may then be graded using the familiar traffic light system:

- Red / high exposure;
- Amber / medium exposure; or
- Green / low exposure.

Red risks generally require an immediate response from management as those related issues potentially present a high exposure to the organisation. The required actions may also extend beyond local management to also include the board of directors. For example, issues around funding a significant deficit in a defined benefit pension scheme might require additional financial resources beyond what is available to the business unit itself.

Amber risks are those that require eventual remediation from local management. They are unlikely to have a significant impact beyond the specific business unit affected. For example, additional certainty over the cost of imported raw materials can be achieved by adopting a more extensive hedging policy than what was currently implemented by the business unit. Although this recommendation might be important to the future profitability of the business unit, it might be unlikely to significantly impact on its ability to continue as a going concern.

Green risks are generally those where the remediation actions suggested to local management are optional. These issues are unlikely to be significant, even for the individual business unit. For example, suggested improvements around the counting of petty cash. It should be noted that including such optional recommendations may cause 'noise' in the report, such that the more important observations are drowned out. Care should therefore be taken on whether to even include this 'nice to have' commentary if that dilutes the actual areas of concern.

Alternatively, on the assumption that all recommendations should be adopted (and that optional recommendations are, therefore, not necessarily relevant for a risk management process), the following classification can instead be used:

- significant design changes;
- limited design changes; or
- documentation matters.

Significant Changes

Significant changes are required where the existing strategies and controls are deemed not to be adequate to mitigate the related risks. These matters would normally require urgent attention from local management. However the suggested corrective actions, by their nature, would generally have extended implementation timeframes of beyond six months.

For example, where the risk assessment has indicated that recent significant regulatory changes to the operational environment of the business unit have not been considered, the corrective actions of engaging with relevant specialists and developing appropriate mechanisms would extend beyond a number of months.

Limited Changes

Limited changes relate to recommendations where the process is broadly sufficient, but specific or a limited number of gaps have nonetheless been identified. These matters would similarly require attention from local management, but because there is already some system in place, their remediation could be somewhat less urgent.

For example, the design of a payment approval process might need to be enhanced to ensure segregation of potentially conflicting duties. The implementation of the suggested corrective action of layering over an additional level of review and sign-off would usually fall within a three to six-month timeframe.

Documentation Matters

Such changes are required where the implemented processes are designed appropriately such that there are few, if any, potential gaps. The operation of these processes can, however, be improved by enhancing the available documentary evidence. By their nature, such recommendations are usually relatively easy to achieve and within a short timeframe of less than three months.

For example, where operational meetings are already frequently held to discuss strategies for collecting outstanding debts, the process can be improved by documenting the considerations and referring back to the agreed action plans to track the progress and efficacy of the various strategies adopted.

Embedding the Process

Once the implementation phase has been completed at all the business units, the next phase involves the integration of the process into the normal or standardised procedures of each business unit.

Whereas the corporate head office is normally responsible for the design and monitoring of the risk management process, the maintenance and updating of the actual underlying risks and controls should reside with local management. They would normally have early visibility on emerging risks and be best-placed to assess and suggest adequate responses.

In **Chapter 3** we indicated that the overall effectiveness of risk management is greatly enhanced by periodic (and indeed frequent) re-assessments of risk. Local management should therefore incorporate a dedicated agenda item of their monthly or bi-monthly management meetings to the area of risk management.

This can involve a review of the currently documented risks as well as a consideration of any additional information that has come to light to support or contradict the initial assessment of these risks.

We will return to this topic of **updating risk** in the next chapter, but at this point it is important to note the typical change in responsibility for the risk management process.

Initially, it is the board of directors, through the corporate head office, that determines the scope and design of the process. The initial implementation may also be driven by a function at the corporate head office. Once this has been completed, local management take responsibility for updating and maintaining the process. The corporate head office would then be tasked with monitoring compliance and reporting to the board of directors any significant changes and developments. Ultimately, the board of directors may determine to enhance or revise the process through these established mechanisms.

Conclusion

In this chapter we discussed the specific organisational structures and reporting tools that might be created around the implementation of a risk management programme. In the next chapter we will focus on implementation of the actual risk management process itself.

Chapter 6

The Risk Management Process

Introduction

In the preceding chapter we considered some of the aspects relating to the organisational structure of a risk management programme. In this chapter we shall turn to the various phases that form part of the actual implementation of the risk management process.

The following phases or stages are generally present in some form or another throughout a risk management process:

- Identify risk
- Grade risk
- Accept risk
- Aggregate risk
- Control risk, and
- Update risk.

Although each of these phases is discrete and could be considered and completed in turn, the flow of information is not always linear. Feedback loops should be built into the process, such that the outcome from one of the later phases may bear on the initial assessment of an earlier phase. For example, poor results evidenced from the Controlling Risk phase in the current phase would require a re-consideration of the results from the Grading risk phase.

Identifying Risk

We have previously considered the definition of 'risk'. We concluded that it broadly relates to negative uncertainty in respect of eventual outcomes. In an enterprise or business context, this encompasses normally all of the activities in which the organisation engages.

These business activities occur at a corporate or head office level as well as at the operational level. The structure of the organisation would inform which of the business units or departments (for smaller organisations) are relevant for risk identification purposes. Dormant or intermediate holding companies (with no employees) would typically not be relevant. Transactions that are routed through these entities are normally controlled elsewhere.

An organisation should carefully determine the appropriate scope of the risk identifying process. It may determine that certain business units have such low trading or balance sheet activity that any risks residing there would invariably be immaterial to the overall organisation. However, as identifying risk is primarily concerned with unknown or unexpected activity, it may be prudent to scope most, if not all, of the business units in the organisation. This is especially the case where a business unit may have 'off-balance sheet' exposures such as potentially onerous leases, legal claims or derivative trading activities.

Scoping

A 'business unit' does not necessarily refer to a separate statutory entity only. Groups may be organised along divisional lines, rather than legal structures. Therefore, organisations should make use of the reporting structures in determining the in-scope business units. As a starting point, the management reporting used by the chief decision-maker (normally the managing director) of the organisation could be used.

Where such reports include information from diverse businesses or across multiple jurisdictions, it may be appropriate to disaggregate the report structure into multiple business units. Ultimately, a relevant business unit would typically have some level of homogenous activity in a single or limited number of jurisdictions. As mentioned above, this may require single legal entities to be classified as separate business units in terms of risk assessment. For example, a division containing a central finance and human resource function, a manufacturing plant and a stand-alone service department, may be analysed as three separate business units depending on the independence of each function.

For very large organisations made up from numerous, individually insignificant business units, it might be a logistical challenge to complete a risk assessment for each entity. The board of directors might then determine to scope in only a certain number of business units that represent a large portion of coverage of the organisation. There are not necessarily any fixed percentages as to what constitutes a large enough portion, but organisations would typically aim to achieve in excess of 50%.

The coverage is normally calculated based on revenue as a proxy for the size and importance of the business unit. Care should however be taken, as a large revenue number would not necessarily indicate a high risk entity. For example, a business unit that is engaged in property development would typically have a significant balance sheet rather than a high rental income. In fact, a low level of turnover might be more indicative of risk as the business unit might be unable to sell or rent out its developments.

Another method is to base the scoping on profit before tax numbers. Again, such an approach might ignore those business units close to breakeven or even loss-making, which would not be consistent with their risk profiles.

As an alternative, the board might determine that the scoping should be performed on a rotational basis. Each business unit would therefore eventually be included in the scoping and then revisited within a specific timeframe. The major concern with this approach is that significant risks might have emerged in the intervening period at those out-of-scope business units. In addition, the board would still need to determine a way to identify which business units to include in the scoping in the current year.

A far more robust approach is where the board of directors develops a number of criteria that, when viewed together, allow for the highest risk business unit to be identified and included in the scoping. The pre-determined criteria that could be used include business units with the following:

- industry-specific developments (such as the downturn in construction activity);
- current year variances (upwards and downwards) of revenue or profit in excess of 20%;
- recent acquisitions or business expansions;
- significant changes in senior management;
- changes in regulatory environments; and
- adverse external audit findings.

Business units could be ranked based on the number of criteria that they meet in order to identify the highest risk entities. In addition to the rankings, the board might also randomly select supposed lower risk business units and review the results from their risk assessment to ensure that the existing pre-determined criteria continues to be robust enough to identify the highest risk business units.

Gathering Information

Once the organisation as a whole has been analysed into its relevant business units or departments, each of these are then targeted for risk identification. There are a number of methods whereby management can gather information about the risks at these business units. For example:

- questionnaires;
- self-assessments, and
- interviews.

Questionnaires The use of questionnaires may be appropriate where there are a significant number of relevant business units, or where time is tight or resources constrained. A centralised corporate head office function, such as risk management, legal or internal audit would typically draft the questionnaire and circulate it to all the affected business units. The questionnaire would usually contain a checklist of expected risks prevalent throughout the organisation, together with acceptable or suggested responses. It would also provide for an open or free-form section where local management can provide an explanation of any other risks not identified in the checklist. It is normally necessary to include some instructions or proposed model answers to try to ensure a level of consistency in the replies from local management.

The level of instruction required would be driven by the familiarity of local management with the concepts of corporate governance in general and risk management in particular. Also, issues around the interpretation of the questions may arise where business units are located in jurisdictions where English is not the normal language used for communication. Management may be somewhat reluctant to fully engage with the process in the absence of training or an explanation of the ultimate goals of the process from the corporate head office.

Furthermore, and depending on the diversity of the organisation, a significant number of questions may be redundant for the vast majority of the business units. For example, a questionnaire that is designed with a manufacturing plant in mind would include a broad range of questions that may be irrelevant to a service department or distribution depot. Local management would, however, still be expected to work through all the questions to ascertain which of them may be applicable. This might place an excessive time burden on them, which would, in turn, undermine the robustness of the entire process.

Another major drawback of the questionnaire approach is that participants may feel constrained in their replies or simply view the process as another paper-filling exercise, without necessarily appreciating its broader aims. Also, their responses may revert back to the model answers where they find the structure of the questionnaires too rigid to be meaningfully applied to their business units.

It is highly likely that follow-up questions, or even interviews, would be required to explore unique or unusual risks identified through the questionnaires. This may of course also result in extensive delays in the overall implementation of the process.

An example of a risk assessment questionnaire is set out below:

EXAMPLE: EXTRACT FROM A RISK ASSESSMENT QUESTIONNAIRE

...

54. Is there a specific regulatory regime governing the activities of your business unit? ☐ ☐ ☐

54.1 If yes, do you engage with external legal counsel to identify changes in regulations?

54.2 Has the regulator visited or assessed your business unit during the last 12 months?

54.3 Has your business unit been fined by the regulator during the last five years?

55. Have there been instances of fraud at your business unit during the last 12 months? ☐ ☐ ☐

55.1 If yes, what is the estimated value of the losses incurred?

55.2 Were investigations launched when the fraud was identified?

55.3 Have any employees been dismissed as a result of the investigations?

56. Are there any other risks applicable to your business unit not already included? ☐ ☐ ☐

56.1 Please provide details of the steps taken by the business unit to address these risks

...

Self-assessments Self-assessments are where the local management team of each relevant business unit completes essentially free-form documents outlining the risks that they have identified by themselves. This approach is likely to result in a more in-depth analysis of risk than could have been achieved with the questionnaires approach. Typically, the self-assessment approach may be appropriate where the business units have traditionally operated without much guidance or oversight from the corporate head office. They may, therefore, have already adopted corporate governance guidelines themselves and incorporated a risk assessment process as part of their standards procedures.

Other advantages of the self-assessment approach are that it is quick to implement and should result in minimal duplication or push-back from the business units. It does, however, assume that all the business units have broadly the same level of sophistication with regards to corporate governance and risk management.

The corporate head office would, in any case, still be required to provide detailed instructions on how this particular assessment should be completed. In particular, they should provide guidance on the extent and depth of the assessment. For example, a business unit involved in construction activities may in the past have focussed on operational and project delivery risks without necessarily considering financial or business continuity risks. Also, issues that might be considered significant risks for a particular business unit may be immaterial for the organisation as a whole.

The major difficulty with the self-assessment approach is, however, to achieve an adequate level of consistency in the responses from all the participants across the organisation. It would be dependent on each of the business units to follow the instructions from the corporate head office although their established approaches may be different. Corporate head office may also then find it challenging to aggregate all the various responses and reporting methods into a single group- or organisation-wide for consideration and review by the board of directors.

Further follow-up questions or interviews may in any case be required to explore any of the unexpected risks identified through the self-assessments. Indeed, it may also be difficult for the corporate head office to give recommendations or suggest alternate strategies in the absence of such follow-up interviews.

Direct Interviews Interviews with members of management from the business units are perhaps the most effective method for gathering information about relevant risks. This usually requires staff of the Risk Management Department (or whomever from the designated corporate head office functions mentioned in **Chapter 5**) to visit each of the relevant business units and conduct face-to-face interviews with key management.

The interviews should all follow a standardised approach to ensure consistency. It would require the interviewers to have already gathered at least some background information on the business units and generated a 'desktop' list of expected risks. This list of expected risks would normally be shared with local management in advance of the meetings to provide a useful framework in which the interviews could be conducted. Some of the expected risks from the 'desktop' review may, of course, ultimately prove to be irrelevant and, similarly, additional risks may emerge from the interviews with local management of the business unit.

The quality and extent of the background information is, however, critical in the preparation of the 'desktop' list of expected risks. Such information can normally be gathered from the following sources:

- broad economic developments in that jurisdiction;
- industry-related publications;

- research papers by third parties;
- strategic vision and goals of the business unit;
- recent financial statements;
- management letters from external auditors;
- internal process and procedure notes;
- monthly or quarterly trading updates;
- internal self-assessments;
- press releases; and
- reports from the applicable regulatory authority.

The interviews would necessarily provide a mechanism whereby participants can offer their own views on applicable risks in real-time. The interviewers can interpret the comments and formulate the responses within the pre-established parameters of the interview. This would ensure that the results are consistent across all the business units and greatly reduce the need for subsequent follow-up interviews to clarify initial responses.

The interviews are also suited for explaining the rationale and background to the risk management programme being implemented. The interviewers are then able to address any questions or concerns that local management may have in this respect.

The biggest drawback of this approach is the requirement for extensive resources in personnel where business units are visited in parallel or, alternatively, a relatively delayed implementation process where each business unit is visited sequentially. This drawback might be overcome by co-opting personnel from the internal audit and legal departments or alternatively considering outsourcing part of the process to third party providers.

Risk Register

The risks that are generated from the 'desktop' review together with those additional ones gathered from the relevant business units can be captured on a '**risk register**'. The risk register allows for a common approach to naming and classifying risk throughout the whole organisation. This will also ensure that the risks from each business unit can be meaningfully and effectively aggregated into the eventual group-wide risk register. We will return to this topic as part of the section on 'Aggregating Risk' later in this chapter.

We discussed in **Chapter 3** the rationale for stratifying risks by their response types. On the risk register, a standardised numbering system could then be used to identify each of these risks separately. For example:

- External risks – number E1, E2, etc.
- Hybrid risks – number H1, H2, ... etc.

External risks are those that largely fall outside of the control of management or where management can only control their 'impact' and not their 'likelihood' (see **Chapter 3**). For example:

- E1 – global and domestic recessions
- E2 – changes in legislation and regulations
- E3 – foreign currency rate fluctuations
- E4 – loss of significant customers
- E5 – competitors and new market entrants.

Hybrid risks are those risks that can, to some extent at least, be influenced by management or where management can control their 'likelihood', but not necessarily their 'impact'. For example:

- H1 – shareholder revolt
- H2 – deficit in defined benefit pension scheme
- H3 – availability of financing facilities
- H4 – sourcing of raw materials
- H5 – technological advances.

Note that in some organisations, where management might be able to exert a higher degree of control over risks classified as external or hybrid above, such risks may be included under internal risks instead.

Because **internal risks** (generally, those risks whose likelihood and impact both fall within the control of management) tend to be significantly more numerous that the other two categories, a system of sub-stratification may be appropriate. For example:

- Strategic risks – number S1, S2, ... etc.
- Fraud risks – number F1, F2, ... etc.
- Legal and contractual risks – number L1, L2, ... etc.
- Financial integrity risks – number N1, N2, ... etc.
- Operational risks – number O1, O2, ... etc.

- Human resource risks – number U1, U2, ... etc.
- Information risk – number I1, I2, ... etc., and
- Reputational risks – number R1, R2, ... etc.

Strategic risks are those risks of particular significance or importance, and normally arise from the strategic goals of the individual business unit or the organisation as a whole. For example:

- S1 – succession planning for senior management positions
- S2 – acquisitions of businesses in existing industries
- S3 – acquisitions of businesses in unrelated industries
- S4 – geographical diversification
- S5 – exit from uneconomic ventures.

Fraud risks, due to their nature and inherent pervasiveness, normally warrant separate identification. By listing out the various types of fraud, each as a unique risk, the responses can be more effectively considered. For example:

- F1 – theft of company assets
- F2 – improper capitalisation of expenditure
- F3 – falsification of expense claims
- F4 – fictitious recording of sales transactions
- F5 – bribery or corrupt acts.

Legal risks typically arise from the negotiation of contracts and other actions that expose the business unit or the organisation as a whole to litigation. For example:

- L1 – side arrangements (or terms omitted from the signed version)
- L2 – existing or pending litigation involving the organisation
- L3 – unresolved and potential warranty claims
- L4 – complexity of contractual arrangements and terms
- L5 – enforceability of contracts in foreign jurisdictions.

Financial integrity risks relate to the accuracy of the periodic internal management reporting packs or annual financial statements. As described in **Chapter 2**, this area was the main focus of the Sarbanes–Oxley Act (2002) in the United States, but is also highly relevant for a broader risk management programme. For example:

- N1 – validity of assumptions used in pension models
- N2 – recoverability of carrying values of assets
- N3 – inappropriate posting of non-standard journals

- N4 – valuation of intangible or derivative assets
- N5 – understatement of liabilities or losses incurred.

Operational risks arise from the normal business activities of the organisation. For example:

- O1 – breakdown in global or local supply chain
- O2 – business continuity or disaster recovery
- O3 – timely project delivery or execution
- O4 – product recalls or product liability
- O5 – quality of sub-contractors or suppliers.

Human resource risks relate to all aspects of hiring, managing and terminating employees. For example:

- U1 – market-related compensation packages
- U2 – balanced scorecard performance management
- U3 – consistent hiring and promotion practices
- U4 – health and safety at the workplace
- U5 – restructuring and terminating employees.

Information risks revolve primarily around the information technology (IT) used by the business unit or the organisation as a whole. For example:

- I1 – change management for IT applications
- I2 – user access to networks, applications and databases
- I3 – backup and restoration of transactional databases
- I4 – implementation of new IT applications
- I5 – theft of confidential business information.

Reputational risks are mostly associated with the brand of the business unit or organisation as a whole. For example:

- R1 – adverse media reporting
- R2 – regulatory penalties and fines
- R3 – industrial action or environmental campaigns
- R4 – labour practices in foreign jurisdictions
- R5 – unauthorised use of brands and trademarks.

The risk population (being the total number of risks relevant to the organisation) will likely be different between business units within the same organisation and, of course, between different organisations – even those that operate in the same industry or market segment. For consistency, this sub-stratification of the risk population into the various risk captions as outlined above should be done from the perspective of the organisation as a whole, especially for the risks considered to be 'strategic' in nature.

Number of Risks Identified

The absolute number of risks that appear on the risk register is highly dependent on the nature, complexity and size of each business unit. An organisation should try to strike a balance between an over-elaborate and unmanageable list of risks at one extreme, and an overly truncated list, from which it would be difficult to pinpoint exact responsibilities, at the other.

As a rough guide, a fully trading business unit in a relatively complex industry, operating in a single jurisdiction would, generally speaking, have around 30 to 40 risks.

Where the number of risks exceeds 50 to 60 there is likely to be too much detail for the board of directors to meaningfully review; they may require a summary of key risks, in any case. The quality of such a summary would then be dependent on the author of the report, which introduces another layer of interpretation, whereby potentially significant risks might be omitted.

On the other hand, a list of, say, 20 risks or less might result in risks with important differentiating characteristics all being amalgamated together. For example, for acquisitive organisations, it might be important to draw a distinction between the controls surrounding the acquisition of a business in an industry very familiar to the organisation and the acquisition of a business in a new, unrelated industry. For the latter scenario, there might be an additional level of oversight required or use made of third-party industry research and valuation specialists. Such additional controls might not be necessary or efficient where the organisation is just consolidating its existing market position by acquiring direct competitors.

It may be difficult for an organisation to anticipate the 'correct' number of risks in advance. Therefore, as outlined in **Chapter 5**, a pilot location might be used to sense-check (and possibly adjust and adapt) the initial expectations. The board of directors then also has an opportunity to review and consider the level of detail of the risk register and whether it is in line with their expectations.

Risk and Control Matrix

Organisations typically link their risk registers with their control environment in a single document, sometimes referred to as a *risk and control matrix*. For example:

EXAMPLE: EXTRACT FROM A RISK AND CONTROL MATRIX

Risk register	Control	
S2: acquisition of business in existing industries	S2.1: approval from board of directors required S2.2: due diligence report from third party specialist S2.3: corporate legal involved in drafting agreement	B L C
E3: foreign currency fluctuations	E3.1: hedging all significant purchases through central treasury function	C
F3: falsification of expense claims	F3.1: approval from line manager before reimburse F3.2: subject to period review by internal audit function	L C
N1: validity of assumptions used in pension models	N1.1: assumptions used mandated by head office N1.2: assumptions benchmarked against industry N1.3: subject to review by internal audit function	C C C
R4: labour practices in foreign jurisdictions	R4.1: corporate code on treatment of workers with abuse reporting mechanism	L

| ... | | |
| ... | | |

Legend

B: board of directors
C: corporate head office
L: local business unit

Corporate Head Office

It is important to include the corporate head office as a business unit for which to indentify risks. Even though a large number of operational risks would generally not be applicable, there are typically a number of risks that reside exclusively at this level of the organisation, along with their key controls and responses. For example, organisations mostly manage and control their pension and share option plans at the corporate level.

In addition, the corporate head office might provide additional control and oversight to certain risk areas that predominantly reside at the local business unit level.

The risk and control matrix normally indicates at which levels of the organisation the particular risk is being managed. This is to ensure that appropriate regard is given to the significant risks. Put another way, the more significant a risk is to the organisation, the more oversight and consultation from management at the corporate head office or board of directors levels is required. As discussed in **Chapter 4**, an organisation can use the authority matrix to help delineate the responsibilities of the local business unit, corporate head office and the board of directors. We will consider this aspect further in the allocating controls section in the next chapter (**Chapter 7**).

Potential Risks

The purpose of identifying risk is not only to capture existing or crystallised risks, but also potential risks based on the currently proposed or expected strategies and plans of the business unit.

Although it may be argued that the scope of such an exercise can in effect be completely open-ended, the resulting potential risks so identified will still be graded for their likelihood of occurrence during the next phase of the process. Therefore, risks that may at the moment appear far-fetched or unrealistic should, nevertheless, be captured and tracked. The actual responses to such potential risks would invariably be at a significantly reduced level to that of risks which already exist. (We will consider the appropriateness of responses in general in the section on controlling risk later in this chapter.)

For example, a business unit may consider that, in response to the recession in their domestic market, an appropriate cost-cutting measure would be to outsource production to a low-cost supplier in another country. If the business unit has not previously operated in that foreign jurisdiction then a number of new potential risks would arise. Even though the decision to outsource may ultimately be based on financial considerations, management of the business unit (and indeed at the corporate head office) should include in their considerations the various new risks that would arise if they decide to proceed. (We will consider this aspect further in the section on accepting risk later in this chapter.)

Grading Risk

Once a complete register of existing and potential risks (based on currently proposed initiatives) has been compiled, the risks need to be graded based on their likelihood of occurrence as well as their potential impact on the business unit.

It is important that risks are graded to ensure the appropriateness of the related responses. Not all of the, say, 40 or so risks would necessarily be of the same significance to the individual business unit or the organisation as a whole.

It is therefore important to define, from the outset, what the increments or tolerances of the grading system are. These tolerances should then be consistently applied to all the business units, irrespective of their size, to ensure consistency of result. For example, a minor business unit (in the overall context of the organisation)

64   *Enterprise Risk Management*

might have a stream of service revenue that is significant to its own operations. However, for the organisation as a whole, that revenue line might not be at all material. That is not to say that the risks associated with the service revenue should be ignored, but that the level of oversight and control required should be proportionally less. The appropriate grading in an organisation-wide context would ensure that those risks reside at the 'local' control level and not necessarily be elevated to require an additional level of oversight by the corporate head office.

Risk Maps

A ***risk map*** is a graphical representation of the interaction between 'likelihood' and 'impact'. It provides a snapshot of the risk profile (being the dispersion of all relevant risk items) of the business unit individually and, when consolidated, of the organisation as a whole.

An organisation should consider the level of calibration used for a risk map. Generally, though a nine-sector risk map is sufficiently detailed (see **Figure 6.1** below). This would imply the following grades:

- Impact – low, medium and high; and
- Likelihood – low, medium and high.

Where high and medium ranges intersect, the sectors might be heavily shaded (or be coloured red) to indicate high overall risk. Where medium and low intersect, the sectors might be medium shaded (or be coloured amber) to indicate medium overall risk. Finally, where medium and low intersect, the sectors might be lightly shaded (or be coloured green) to indicate low overall risk.

It is not unusual to find a scattering of risk items across all of the sectors in the risk map. There is generally, however, a concentration of items around the middle diagonal running from the top left to the bottom right of the risk map.

An example of a risk map for a relatively large and complex business unit could be as shown below in **Figure 6.1**:

Figure 6.1: Inherent Risk Map

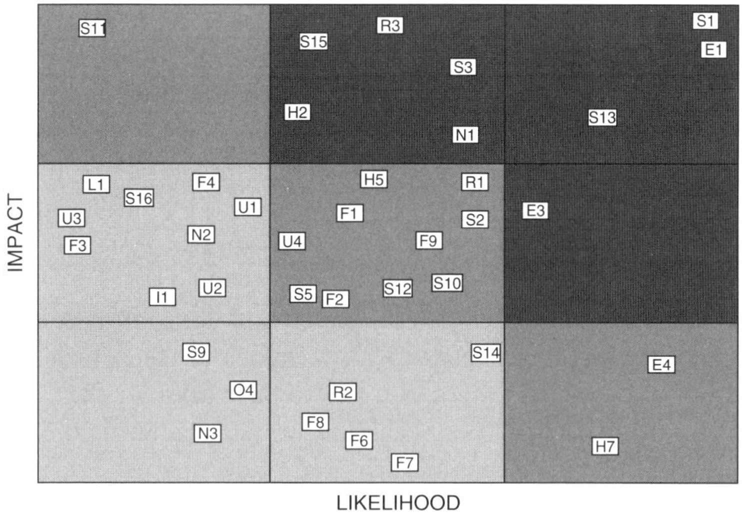

Defining 'Likelihood' and 'Impact'

In the section on likelihood and impact in **Chapter 3**, we outlined some methods that an organisation could use to calculate and define what is meant by 'high', 'medium' and 'low'.

For some risks, such as those around financial integrity, the determination of impact might be relatively straightforward. For example, the theoretical maximum monetary impact of risk '**N2 – recoverability of carrying values of assets**' would be the net carrying amount of those assets (such as debtors or inventory) currently reflected on the balance sheet of the business unit. The assumptions used in calculating the existing impairment provisions (such as the bad debt allowance) might also shed light on the likelihood of write-down occurring. For example, organisations might calculate that the probability of the write-down of €100,000 is 20%, of €250,000 is 50% and of €400,000 it is 30%. The weighted impact would then be estimated at around €265,000; but, inversely, the likelihood could also be calculated as being around 35%.

The risks associated with liabilities typically involve understatement; for example, that the pension deficit might be higher than currently expected because of errors in the assumptions used. The sensitivity analysis that actuaries generally produce as part of their reporting might provide some insight into the possible value of the exposure. Alternatively, historic trends on estimation errors might provide a basis for extrapolation of the current values as well as their likelihood.

For risks such as '**S4 – geographical diversification**', the impact, at least initially, could be calculated with reference to the start-up budget allocated. If the expansion ends in complete failure, then the total value of the investment would probably be lost. The likelihood is more a matter of judgment, based on the experience of peers or the complexity of the local market.

For external risks, such as '**E1 – global and domestic recessions**', the impact might be calculated with reference to the expected contraction in a specific market, e.g. new vehicle sales, or the broader economy-wide decline. The likelihood would be towards the right-hand side of the risk map until such time as the economy is predicted to start expanding again.

For the majority of risks, it might, however, be difficult to exactly pinpoint a value and probability. This is one of the reasons why a nine-sector risk map is most likely to be sufficient for presentational purposes. The more finely calibrated the risk map is, the more difficult it becomes to correctly place the risk items.

It is, in any case, not necessarily of critical importance to precisely calculate values and place the various risk items accordingly. Organisations might effectively and efficiently use alternative techniques to strictly mathematical computations. For example, a 'relative' approach might prove to be just as useful.

Relative Grading Approach

In a 'relative' approach, the preparer uses the positions of the more easily quantifiable risk items, such as the financial integrity risks, as benchmarks for the other risks. The risk map is, therefore, first populated with the positions of those risk items. The preparer then seeks to identify all the risk items that are closely associated with those risks already mapped. For example, the risk of valuation of intangibles might serve as a rough proxy for the risk around the acquisition of new businesses. This in turn might inform the position of the risk on geographical expansion, which is likely to be riskier than a local acquisition.

In order to remove bias, the risk map might be independently completed by various knowledgeable personnel at the corporate head office and then compared and contrasted against one another. Typically, the majority of the risk items would be mapped fairly similarly or within broadly the same map sections. Where, however, the risk items are mapped into significantly different sections, say, for example, low impact, medium likelihood compared to high impact, high likelihood, the preparers might discuss the criteria they used to determine their positions. It might be found that one of the preparers did not have all the information or attached undue weight to a specific issue. In cases where agreement cannot be reached, it is usually prudent to adopt a conservative approach and follow the higher risk map location. For example, the impact of recent or impending regulatory changes might be difficult to ascertain and should therefore be rated higher until such time as sufficient experience or understanding is gained in their operation.

The position of the risk items can be amended throughout the process as additional information becomes available. Similarly, once the risk map has been established in the first year of the risk assessment process it can be used as a benchmark for the following year.

Inherent Risks and Residual Risks

It is also important to draw a clear distinction between inherent risk and residual risk.

An inherent risk map is an illustration of the likelihood and impact of risks *before* considering any of the responses or controls already implemented by the business unit. Put another way, if local management either missed that particular risk or decided not to take any action to mitigate it, then an inherent risk map would indicate the likely impact on the organisation. Figure 6.1 above is an example of an inherent risk map.

Over time, the inherent risk map would change to reflect developments in the broader environment of the business unit. For example, the location of the risk associated with the **global and domestic recessions** (being risk 'E1' in accordance with the naming convention used earlier in this chapter) would have been on a steep upward trajectory since 2008 in most of the developed nations of the world.

A **residual risk map**, on the other hand, illustrates the likely impact of risks *after* taking into account the responses and actions of management of the business unit. An example of that same risk map with a residual risk view might look as follows in **Figure 6.2**:

Figure 6.2: Residual Risk Map

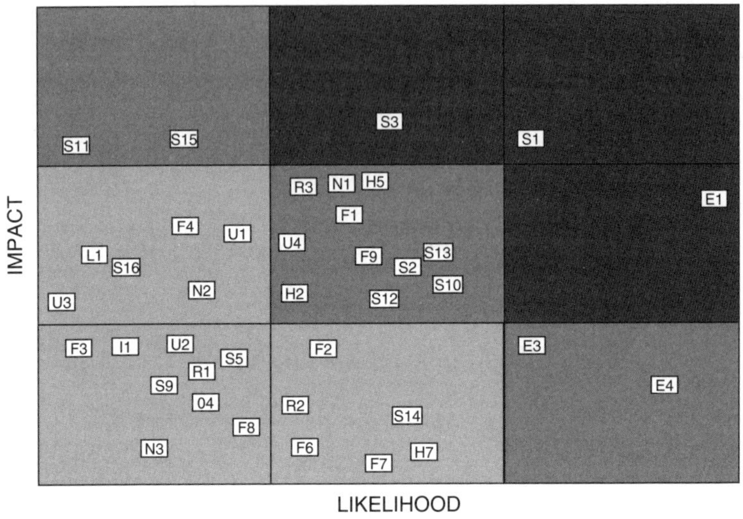

The residual risk map usually indicates a shift in the risk items toward the green sectors. It implies that, through the responses and controls implemented by local management, the likely negative impact of the risks identified has been reduced.

For internal risks, the change in position can typically be both towards the left and downwards, meaning that both their impact and likelihood have been reduced. Hybrid risks ordinarily only move towards the left as their impact is not necessarily within the control of management. External risks, on the other hand, only tend to move downwards, as their likelihood falls outside of the control of management.

Any risks that have not been addressed by management would remain at the same position on the inherent and residual risk maps. The quality or effectiveness of the responses and actions from management can be ascertained by the relative shift in position. For example, inherent risks that fall in the heavily shaded (or red) sectors may be mitigated to such an extent through well-designed and executed controls that at a residual level they fall within a lightly shaded (or green) sector.

The board of directors might, therefore, wish to review both the inherent and residual risk maps of a business unit in conjunction with each other in order to form a complete opinion about the responsiveness of management at that specific location. An inherent risk map viewed in isolation might, on the other hand, provide a distorted picture of the risk profile of a business unit.

An *inherent* risk map with numerous risk items located in heavily shaded (or red) sectors should not in and of itself raise concern. It would merely serve to emphasise the need for management to remain vigilant and focus their minds on developing appropriate responses. A *residual* risk map where a significant number of risk items still fall in the heavily shaded (or red) sectors, on the other hand, would indicate a serious exposure for the organisation. The responses to the relevant heavily shaded (or red) sector risks are either inadequately designed to begin with or their implementation and execution is non-existent, inconsistent or flawed.

In order to specify exactly where the responses and actions are breaking down, an organisation can determine to present **two stages of residual risk maps**:

- initial (or design effectiveness) residual map; and
- final (or operating effectiveness) residual map.

A similar level of judgment is required in positioning the risk items on either of the residual risk maps as placing them on the inherent risk map.

Initial Residual Risk Map

For the initial residual risk map, the preparer takes account of the results of the walkthrough performed to ascertain the design effectiveness of the controls. In respect of strategies, the preparer considers the robustness and reasonableness of the goals and plans to determine whether the inherent risk has been reduced. (In **Chapter 7**, we will discuss in further detail the different techniques used to monitor controls and strategies.)

Effectively designed controls and strategies would result in the positions of the risk items moving left and downwards (towards the lightly shaded or green sectors) in accordance with the type of risk as outlined above. When determining the location of the risk items, the preparer would normally assume that the controls and strategies actually operate as designed. Therefore, the initial residual risk map would show the lowest level to which the risk items have been reduced. Put another way, it should display the most favourable view of risk mitigation.

For example, the following initial risk map (shown in **Figure 6.3** below) indicates the relative movement in the positions of risk items for various possible scenarios:

- Risk E1 – the strategy is reasonably designed, but only able to reduce a portion of the impact.
- Risk E3 – the strategy is non-existent and therefore has no bearing on the impact.
- Risk H2 – the strategy is reasonably designed and almost completely removes the likelihood.
- Risk H5 – the strategy is unrealistic and therefore has no bearing on the likelihood.
- Risk S1 – the controls are designed effectively to almost completely remove both impact and likelihood.
- Risk S2 – the control is designed effectively, although it reduces impact, rather than likelihood.

Figure 6.3: Movement of Risk Items from the Inherent Risk Map to the Initial Residual Risk Map

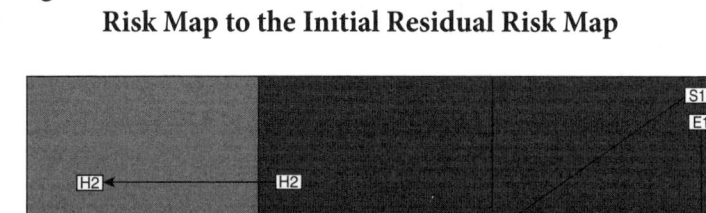

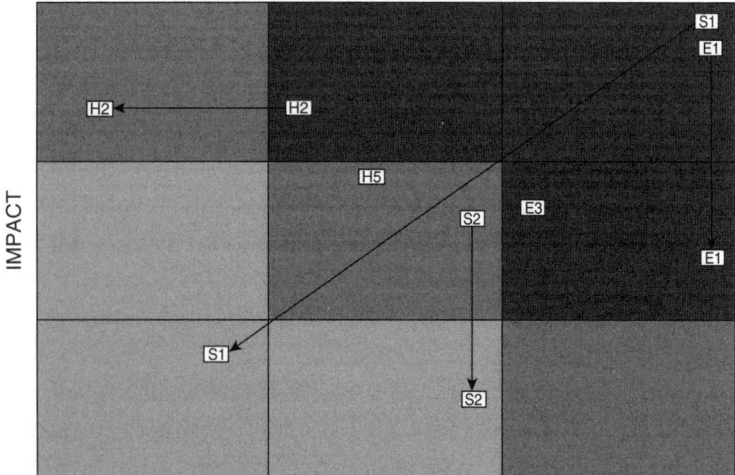

Final Residual Risk Map

For the final residual risk map, the preparer also takes account of the result of the testing performed on the operating effectiveness of the controls. In respect of strategies, the actual results from the key performance indicators or milestones are considered to determine whether the overall goals are being achieved. (We will return to these areas as part of the next chapter.)

Effectively operating controls and strategies, being those that perform fully in accordance with their design, would result in the position of the risk item remaining unchanged from that of the initial residual risk map. This is because the initial residual risk map is prepared on the assumption that the controls and strategies would, in fact, operate as designed.

If, however, the result of the testing of operational effectiveness reveals control failures or strategies that are not achieving their milestones, then the position of the risk items would move back towards their positions on the inherent risk map.

Whether the location of the risk item on the final residual risk map returns to its starting position (per the inherent risk map) is dependent on the nature and extent of the failure of its associated controls and strategies. In particular, if the risk is mitigated by a number of controls, then even if one were found not to be effective, the others might compensate for that failure. In such a scenario, the final position would be somewhere along the continuum between the 'inherent' position and the 'initial residual' position. Similarly, the closer a strategy is to its pre-determined milestones and key performance indicators, the closer the position of the risk item would be to the 'initial residual' position.

The following final residual risk map (see **Figure 6.4** below) indicates the relative movement in the positions of risk items for various possible outcomes:

- Risk E1 – the strategy has only achieved some of its milestones and key performance indicators.
- Risk E3 – the strategy is non-existent and therefore no monitoring or verification was performed.
- Risk H2 – the strategy is achieving all of its milestones and key performance indicators.
- Risk H5 – the strategy is unrealistic and therefore no monitoring or verification was performed.

72 *Enterprise Risk Management*

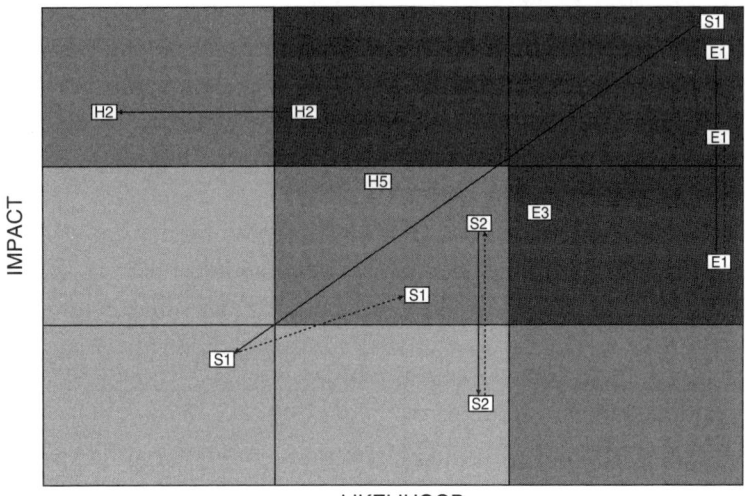

Figure 6.4: Final Residual Risk Map

- Risk S1 – the testing of the operational effectiveness of the controls indicated some failures, but the remaining controls compensated to some extent.
- Risk S2 – the testing of the operational effectiveness of the only associated control resulted in a fail. As there were no other compensating controls associated to this risk, its impact on the organisation returned to its inherent level.

Accepting Risk

In **Chapter 3,** we briefly discussed classifying risks to reflect the risk acceptance of the organisation. This requires the risk register to be analysed as follows:

- unavoidable risk;
- avoidable risk; and
- future risk.

We indicated that the majority of risks on the risk register would invariably be unavoidable. In that sense, the organisation has no option but to address these risks or accept the likely impact (per the inherent risk map) of taking no action at all.

Certain risks are, however, avoidable in the sense that some of the strategies either currently engaged in or proposed for the future are optional.

For example, the risk related to **acquisitions of businesses in existing industries** and the risk related to **acquisitions of businesses in unrelated industries** (being risks 'S2' and 'S3' respectively, in the naming convertion used earlier in this chapter) are generally avoidable, as an organisation could determine to only grow its business organically. In that sense, all issues regarding, for example, an unfamiliar regulatory environment or valuation concerns surrounding new businesses can be classified as avoidable risks.

Where the board of directors determine that a specific avoidable risk is unacceptable, senior management should implement controls to prevent or prohibit the scenario that gives rise to the risk from occurring. For example, where it is determined that taking out speculative derivative instruments (such as interest ratio swaps or credit default swaps) is deemed to introduce unacceptable risks to the organisation, the relevant procedures manual should be updated to reflect the prohibition of such transactions, along with a training and monitoring programme to ensure compliance. Changes to the trading mandates lodged with financial institutions might also be required to prevent or, at a minimum, detect breaches of the new policy.

Determining which risks are avoidable and which ones are not is, however, still a matter of significant professional judgment for the board of directors. The following area of ideas might be a useful guide to them when exercising this judgement:

- corporate risk appetite;
- source of risks;
- interaction with existing risks; and
- future risks.

Corporate Risk Appetite

Risk appetite refers, in a sense, to the aggressiveness of the organisation in pursuing its vision.

As discussed earlier in **Chapter 4**, the corporate vision is that statement from which all further strategies, goals and objectives should ultimately be derived. In that sense, it can be seen as the very reason for the existence of the organisation. As such, all strategies, controls and actions of management should, in some way, enhance the cause of the organisation and so move it closer to achieving its vision.

Of course, a vision might be 'closed', such that the organisation is wound up once that specific vision has been achieved. For our purposes, however, we will consider the much more common 'open-ended' vision. In that context, a vision is not necessarily ever fully attainable, but a constant moving and, in fact, receding 'goal line'. For example, where an organisation has achieved market leadership in a specific segment as envisaged, the vision is normally then amended to focus on maintaining that position in perpetuity.

As such, the vision is also a key piece of infrastructure underpinning the entire risk management system. Although it might, and indeed should, be set at a high-level, it is of critical importance that it is appropriately reviewed and assessed by the board of directors.

As discussed, from the vision, initially the broad strategies and finally the individual goals and action plans of the organisation are distilled. The risk management system would then similarly have to operate in this context. The risk appetite would inform the means and methods that an organisation employs to achieve its vision.

The strategies might be set at an aggressive level when that reflects the risk appetite. For example, the strategy may call for double-digit growth rates in revenue or profitability. The tactical responses to such a strategy might similarly require expansion into unusual markets, using extensive leverage or under-investment in back-office systems. The board need to be aware that by setting that particular risk appetite they are also accepting the risks that flow from the tactical responses.

There is an old adage that states "the higher the risk, the higher the return". The reverse might be equally, if not more, true in that "the higher the return, the higher the risk". Targets that are set too aggressively might perversely cause managers to engage in unacceptable risks. The board are ultimately responsible for ensuring that the appropriate balance between these competing forces is achieved. (This might be done as part of the fraud risk assessment process, as described in **Chapter 9**.)

The board of directors also need to take note that the risk appetite might change and develop over the course of the evolution of the organisation and the broader industry in which it operates.

For example, at the end of the last century, a majority of start-up technology firms determined that growth in market share or the top-line revenue numbers were of paramount importance. They therefore set their corporate visions accordingly. Those visions and the more detailed strategies flowing from them significantly downplayed the importance of profitability (at least in the short term) and cash flow. For that industry, in particular, it was ultimately proved to be largely an unsustainable strategy resulting in the so-called 'dotcom crash'.

That said, an organisation might reasonably determine that during its first couple of years of existence, it is appropriate to gain market share at the expense of high margins. Over time, as the organisation or its market becomes more mature, the vision and strategies can change accordingly to focus more on working capital management. Ultimately, when the market is fully saturated, the focus can change again to cost control (but perhaps also innovation to create new markets). The risk appetite would then, similarly, have changed from being aggressive (higher risk) to moderate and finally conservative (lower risk).

Thus, assessing the risk appetite of an organisation might provide useful insights to the board of directors on which risks are acceptable for the organisation to take on.

The Source of Risks

The base cause or source of the identified risks may provide another good indication as to whether those risks are avoidable or not.

In determining whether to accept a particular internal risk, the board of directors should ask why that risk is, in fact, applicable to the organisation. Or, put another way, what action, if any, could the organisation take that would remove the risk from the risk register altogether?

The simple answer to this question would most likely be that the identified risks are the direct result of merely being in business (e.g. financial integrity risks) and would therefore tend to be unavoidable.

On the other hand, some risks may be the result of doing business in a specific, regulated industry or in a foreign jurisdiction. In that sense the identified risks resulting from the decision to operate in, say, a specific jurisdiction are avoidable should the organisation chose to disinvest from that country.

Isolating and then understanding what the causes are of those avoidable risks will be relevant to the board in order for them to determine the appropriate action. In short, the board would need to weigh the impact and likelihood of the avoidable risks against their expected returns for the organisation.

In the past for the organisation, the expected returns might have been higher and the resultant risks therefore acceptable. For example, the high risks surrounding the development of rural land into housing estates might have compensated for by the prospect of significant profit opportunities in an environment of easily available credit. This consideration might have encouraged the organisation to enter that particular market, even though their core business would have been pure contracting work or completely unrelated to the building trade. As a result of the recent 'credit crunch', the balance between those avoidable risks and their rewards would have to have been re-evaluated. The revised profitability forecasts, for example, around finding buyers to off-load completed estates in a saturated market, may no longer have been sufficient to compensate for the associated risks of being burdened by excessive inventory of unsold properties. The avoidable risks might therefore have become unacceptable.

The board of directors might then have to decide what the best course of action is to extricate the organisation from those risks and minimise its future exposures.

Interaction with Existing Risks

However, the mere fact that a risk is avoidable does not necessarily mean that it should be avoided. An organisation might be forced to engage in 'optional' strategies, because its traditional business is under threat. For example, risk in respect of **technological advances** (being the risk classified as **'H5'** in accordance with the naming convention earlier in this chapter) might have the potential to completely destroy the organisation's current product line and so prompt renewed investment in research and development or strategic acquisitions.

Similarly, a saturated home market might force an organisation to add, say, risk **'S4 – geographical diversification'** by expanding internationally. Where the board then decides to avoid the risks associated with setting up in a foreign jurisdiction, they might find, on the other hand, that residual grading of risk **'E4 – loss of significant customers'** has now become unacceptably high. In such circumstances, the board might be required to opt for the 'lesser of two evils' – understanding that the alternative is ultimately less acceptable.

In reality, the options presented to the board are not necessarily as clearly demarcated or binary as in this example. Typically, various initiatives are presented in conjunction with one another. For example, a cost-cutting programme in the domestic market is tied together with a marketing drive and price reductions. Similarly, the international expansion might be done in progressive stages of first employing a local agent, then opening a branch or taking an equity stake in a local firm before proceeding to invest in a full-blown local subsidiary. In that way, the board is not hitching the entire future of the organisation to a single decision – 'betting the farm', so to speak. By gradually increasing the investment and exposure to that which the management experience gained from doing business there, the balance of risk and reward flowing from the expansion might become more acceptable to the organisation.

The board of directors might also reasonably determine that some of the avoidable risks actually act as natural hedges against some of the other risks. For example, embracing and focussing on effectively mitigating risk **'S5 – exit from uneconomic ventures'** as an option for any of its current or future businesses might allow the board to be more aggressive in its acquisitions, the rationale being that at least some purchases are invariably going to fall below expectation and that by not recognising failure early and having an appropriate exit plan, significant opportunities might be foregone and resources wasted.

Future or Potential Risks

As discussed above, the risk register can act as an early warning system to highlight the expected risks should a proposed new initiative be implemented. It is perhaps significantly easier for an organisation to make its determination on whether to accept future risks or not when compared to the challenges facing an organisation having to deal with relating to existing risks. For example, there is likely to be only limited collateral impact from declining to proceed with a new initiative (and thereby avoiding some future risks altogether) in contrast to winding up an established operation (and having to mitigate against the risks that crystallised from that decision).

78   *Enterprise Risk Management*

That said, there might also be significant opportunity costs in attempting to avoid future risks. The board might be too conservative and miss out on reasonable growth areas by refusing to engage in new initiatives. Again, the board should ideally try to isolate and understand the future risks and compare those against the expected rewards. Where they decide to proceed with the new strategy they might set down markers or future points, at which time the perceived benefits would again be weighed against the related risks.

To facilitate this, some organisations carry out a mini risk assessment process for each major new initiative. They adopt the exact same phases and principles as for the overall risk management programme, thus ensuring that the same level of diligence is attached to new strategies and that 'empire-building' or expansion purely for its own sake is avoided in the organisation.

Aggregating Risk

Once all the risks have been identified and graded across the various business units, it is necessary to aggregate them together to form the overall risk register and risk map for the organisation as a whole.

Overall Risk Register

Provided that a consistent numbering system was used for all the various risk items across the business units, the overall risk register should then be a simple aggregation of the individual risk registers.

The overall risk register would typically only list the name of the risk items, and, perhaps, the names of the business units where they are applicable. It would not detail all of the individual responses as these would tend to be too voluminous to be reviewed at a meaningful level. In any case, the board would already have reviewed and considered the appropriateness of the responses of each individual business unit.

If required, however, the overall risk register may contain a reference to the highest level in the organisation where each risk is being managed. This may be useful as a final 'sense check' that due regard is being given to the significant risks, especially when reviewed in conjunction with the overall risk map. As discussed in **Chapter 7**, the general rule of thumb is that the more significant a risk is to the organisation, the more and higher level of oversight it demands. The board of directors should therefore expect a correlation between inherent risks falling in the heavily shaded (or 'red') sectors of the risk map and those risks that are being managed at a corporate and board level.

Risk Template

A risk template (as distinct from the risk register) may provide a useful alternative tool for the board of directors. Whereas the risk register can be seen as a vertical (per business unit) analysis of risk, the risk template, on the other hand, provides a horizontal (per risk) analysis. This means that for every risk item, the various responses from each of the applicable business units are aggregated. This allows the board to review how each specific risk is being managed across the organisation, instead of how each business unit is responding to its risks. The overall risk register is a single document listing all the risks of the organisation. The number of individual risk templates would reflect the number of individual risks per the risk register.

As discussed in **Chapter 4**, the department or function tasked with the implementation of the risk management programme can use various tools to capture the information gathered throughout the process. Because the preparation of the risk templates is essentially just the slicing and presenting of the same information as contained on the individual risk registers in a different format, a database might be particularly useful in this regard.

The risk template typically contains the following headings:

- risk item and name;
- risk description;
- overall conclusions; and
- analysis of responses.

The **risk item and name** should be the same as those used on the individual and overall risk registers to ensure consistency.

The **risk description** allows for a more detailed discussion about the nature of the specific risk and might even include some additional information from independent research or experience. For example, the risk related to **bribery and corruption** (being risk **'F5'**, per the naming convention used earlier in this chapter) might include results from a recent country-specific survey on the perceived prevalence of corruption in each jurisdiction to allow the board to consider the adequacy of the responses of the business units in that context. Such contextual information would typically have been shared with local management already during the identifying risk phase to help them to develop the necessary controls and strategies.

The **overall conclusions** section is usually a free-form section where the risk management department (or other corporate function tasked with the implementation of the risk management programme) can share its own insights or concerns in respect of the specific risk item. It may, for example, highlight significant disparities between the various responses from the applicable business units or that the responses, in general, fall far short of best practice guidelines. The board might pay particular attention to such overall conclusions where they are presented with fairly esoteric risk items.

The **analysis of responses** contains details of the controls and strategies of each applicable business unit. Where such controls and strategies were deemed to be insufficient, the recommendations generated by the risk management department are normally also included. This analysis should allow the board to easily identify whether there is a consistency in the responses from the business units. It should also help to identify internal best practice where one or more business units have developed a particularly efficient response to the risk item. Other business units confronted with the same risk can then be encouraged to implement some or all of the aspects of the responses from the leading business unit. Those other business units can also leverage off the experience of the leading business unit to avoid having to 'reinvent the wheel'. The other business units are considerably more likely to adopt a new response that has already been tried and tested at another business unit, rather than a 'textbook-based' approach that may not be consistent with the culture of those business units.

The analysis should not only include the responses from local management, but also, where applicable, the oversight from the other role players (such as the corporate head office and the board of directors itself).

An example of a risk template might then look as follows in **Figure 6.5**:

Figure 6.5: Example of a Risk Template

H2 Deficit in defined benefit pension schemes

| Likelihood | Impact | Overall |

Description

The turmoil in the financial markets over the previous years has significantly eroded the asset values for all of the pension schemes in the Group. The averages declines of around 32% is, however, slightly better than the overall market (around 41%), mainly due to historic investment strategies that afforded a higher allocation to bonds (around 40%) compared to peers (around 25%).

Notwithstanding this, certain business units were required to make significant additional capital contributions to return their pension schemes to solvency. The level and timing of these contributions varied, depending on the local regulations applicable in their jurisdictions.

Business unit	Strategy or control	Recommendation
Corporate head office	All assumptions used in the calculation of the pension obligations are reviewed for consistency and reasonableness by Group Treasury. Assumptions are benchmarked against those used by three other listed peers	Consider moving to a single actuarial service provider to reduce costs
Business unit A	Current deficit calculated in excess of 50 million. Funding proposal (including small curtailment of benefits) still being developed – finalisation only expected late the third quarter of the current financial year	Pending review of finalised funding proposal
Business unit B	Current deficit estimated at around £2 million Proposal submitted to local pension regulator to make additional quarterly contributions of £0.8 million over next 18 months to close deficit. Approval from regulator expected within the first quarter	Update on approval from regulator
Business unit C	Small deficit of less than €1million (no requirement locally to submit a funding proposal). Scheme is closed now to new entrants. Investment strategy revised to move to 80% gilts over the next three years	None noted
Business unit D	Previous DB scheme converted into a DC scheme four years ago. All associated liabilities settled at the same time	None noted

Note: the shading (or colour coding) attributed to the 'likelihood, impact and overall' cells reflects the position of the H2 risk item on the Overall (residual) risk map (discussed below).

The colour coding attributed to the business units themselves reflects the position of the H2 risk item on their individual risk maps. This is done to allow the board to efficiently pinpoint which specific business units are responsible for contributing to the overall risk item position.

The colour coding or shading attributed to the recommendations reflects their importance or significance (as described in the previous chapter). For example:

- 'Brown' (shown above in **Figure 6.5** with a 'trellis' line background (▩)) indicates that significant changes are required that will only be completed in a timeframe beyond six months.
- 'Orange' (shown above with a vertical line background (||||)) indicates more limited changes that can be implemented within six months (in this case, a request to major actuarial firms to tender for the combined business of the group).
- 'Blue' (shown above with a horizontal line background (≡)) indicates documentation matters only (with no process changes required) and can be expected to be finalised within the next three months.

This colour coding and shading would also provide a benchmark for local management and the board of directors to track the progress made as part of updating the risk assessments for the business units.

Colour coding and shading affords an easy and consistent method for additional information to be succinctly presented in the risk assessment reports.

Overall Risk Maps

Provided that the same calibration was used for the individual risk maps of each business unit, then the overall risk map of the organisation can be created by aggregating all of the individual business unit risk maps together. If all the business units have mapped a specific risk item as having a *low likelihood* and a *medium impact*, then the overall risk map would more than likely also place the risk item in that sector.

A level of judgment is, however, required where the risk map positions of a risk item are dissimilar across the various business units of an organisation. In such a scenario, the 'average point' between all the various individual locations could be used for the overall location. This means that a business unit with the risk item in a green (lightly shaded) sector of their individual risk map could effectively cancel out or mitigate against a business unit with the same risk item in a red (heavily shaded) sector of their individual risk map to give an overall amber (medium shaded) risk location on the overall risk map. Put another way, having more than one business unit could be seen as a risk mitigation response in itself. If the controls failed at Business Unit A then the likely impact would fall within the red sector (heavily shaded). However, because there are other business units (B and D) that are more effectively controlled, it is unlikely that their controls would have failed at the same time. Therefore, the organisation, as a whole, should benefit from the diversification of the responses to that risk, resulting in an overall risk map location in the amber sector (medium shaded). For example:

Figure 6.6: The Relative Position of a Risk Item Across Various Business Units

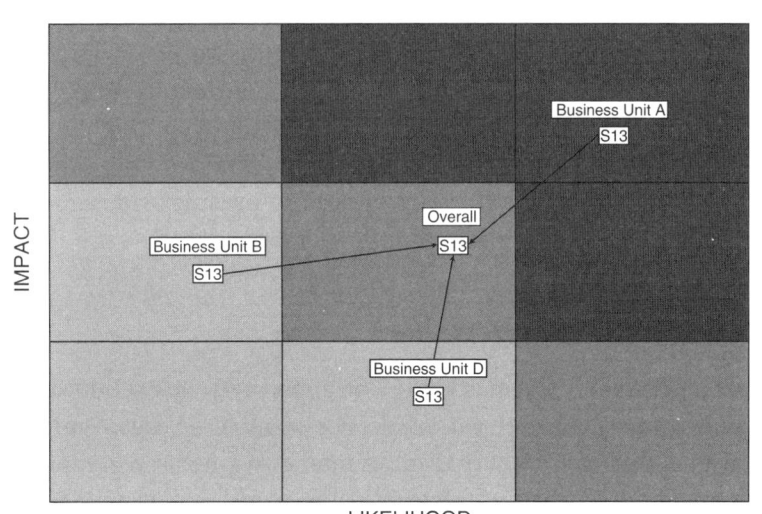

The relative size of each of the business units would not necessarily affect the 'average point' approach. For example, even if Business Unit A was twice the size of Business Units B and D, the mid-point between the risk locations would still be appropriate. This is because consistent calibration (of likelihood and impact) was used in mapping the risk items of each business unit. So if Business Unit A was in the process of executing an acquisition that was double the value of the acquisitions in Business Units B and D, then the risk item on its risk map of Business Unit A would already be much higher on the 'impact' axis. It might, of course, be so elevated in the red sector (heavily shaded) of Business Unit A that the average point between that and all the other business units remains in a red sector, albeit at a slightly reduced likely impact level.

Overall risk maps can be generated at the inherent as well as the residual (initial and final) levels depending on the preference of the board of directors. As discussed above, the board might find it useful to compare and contrast the inherent risk map with the residual risk map of a specific business unit to ascertain the responsiveness of that particular management team to the risks facing the business unit. At the overall level this may prove perhaps less useful, as the information presented would likely be at too high a level. That said, the comparison might still help inform the board where to focus their attention and oversight. For example, where a risk item on the inherent risk map was rated in a red sector, but on the residual (initial) risk map in the green sector (meaning that the relevant controls are effectively designed), the board might determine that it is necessary to pay particular attention to the monitoring of the controls implemented in response to that risk item. The board of directors might rightly be satisfied with the design of those controls, but would still be concerned that those controls would critically need to operate as designed and then also consistently throughout the period required.

Sub-organisational Aggregation

Aggregation may also, on occasion, be appropriate at levels lower than those for the organisation as a whole. For example, an organisation that consists of divisions in very distinct market segments, e.g. those with various manufacturing plants across the world, along with separate servicing and maintenance units, might find it appropriate to aggregate the risk registers from only the manufacturing units together. It might be useful where there are separate executive directors responsible for manufacturing and servicing divisions. Although perhaps only a limited number of risks would be 'shared' across the manufacturing and servicing divisions, the directors responsible might wish to consider their areas separate from the distortions caused by the other division.

This applies equally to where there are divisional head offices below the corporate head office or where a regional board of directors is responsible for all business units, irrespective of market segment, within a specific geography or jurisdiction.

Controlling Risk

Following on from the identification, grading and accepting of risk items, the board should consider the appropriateness of the responses identified to mitigate those risks. These mitigating responses from management can be classified into two somewhat distinct categories:

- controls; and
- strategies.

Controls

Controls are detailed procedures or activities that are implemented by management in response to specific internal risks. These procedures all tend to share the following characteristics:

- detailed description;
- control owner;
- frequency; and
- evidence.

The **detailed description** of a control normally specifies exactly how the control should operate by using verbs such as reconcile, review, vouch and recalculate.

The **control owner** is the person responsible for the execution of the control. Junior employees are usually involved in vouching and reconciliation controls, whereas senior employees or management are involved with review controls.

The **frequency** of when a control is required to operate can range from multiple times a day to an annual basis only. As a general guide, lower level (or transactional) controls tend to operate more frequently than higher level (or review) controls.

Generally, the control owner has to **evidence**, through either a manual or electronic signature that the control operated as required

86   *Enterprise Risk Management*

in its description. Evidence refers to the documentation that is available to support whether a control operated or not.

As a result of these well-defined and clear characteristics, the process of assessing controls and verifying their compliance is also relatively straightforward. In the next chapter, on verifying controls and strategies, we will consider the various possibilities for assurance that the controls have operated as expected and for the intended period.

Risks where controls are normally the appropriate response include:

- F – Fraud risks
- L – Legal and contractual risks
- N – Financial integrity risks
- U – Human resource risks
- O – Operational risks
- I – Information risks.

Strategies

Strategies, on the other hand, are significantly less well-defined than controls and, therefore, more difficult to assess and verify. However, strategies are typically the only available responses to those risks that do not fall within the control of management, i.e. external and hybrid risks.

In addition to those risk varieties, some of the strategic and reputational risks might be so infrequent or variable that it would be difficult to design well-defined controls for testing. For example, the response to risk '**R1 – adverse media reporting**' could be limited to designating an emergency response team that would convene and determine an appropriate next course of action. The uncertainty of what the adverse media reporting might entail would prevent a more detailed or complete action plan. Where an organisation grades the inherent risk of such a media report as particularly high, however, they might in addition perform some scenario planning together with model media statements for each so perceived eventuality. Ultimately though, the effectiveness of these responses cannot be fully assessed or tested until the event actually occurs. In that sense, the responses are not controls for which their compliance can be monitored.

It is important for strategies to be clearly defined. This, in particular, would require the determination of what would constitute the strategy as having been considered a success or not. For example, a standard strategy in response to risk '**E1 – global and domestic**

recessions' is a cost-cutting programme. For assessment purposes, such a programme would be deemed a success if overhead costs are reduced by, e.g. a minimum of 10% over the next year. In the absence of clearly defined targets and timeframes, it would be impossible to either compare the reasonableness of the target itself or to track the progress towards realising that target.

Longer term strategies, e.g. an integration of the back-office functions of separate business units or the migration to a shared service centre, tend to require numerous milestones along the way to achieving the ultimate target. In addition, budgets might need to be established against which to track the expenditure incurred in respect of the strategy.

We will return to these 'project management' techniques to assess the effectiveness of the strategies as part of **Chapter 7**.

Design Effectiveness

As discussed above, the inherent risk map of a business unit reflects the likely impact of risks prior to the consideration of any of its controls or strategies.

The risk management department or function (and ultimately the board of directors) should first determine whether the responses (controls and strategies) are designed, at least on paper, in such a way that they can reasonably be expected to mitigate the corresponding risks.

This is a critical consideration, because controls that operate exactly in accordance with a defective design are still not effective in mitigating risks. Significant resources, such as management time, might be wasted in performing and verifying such controls without necessarily realising any benefit from that.

Controls, in particular, are likely to be mostly at such a detailed level that the board might delegate their design assessment to the risk management department. The design of the strategies, on the other hand, should be reviewed and assessed at board level, given their potential demand on resources of the organisation as well as their far-reaching impact.

The following criteria might be helpful in specifically considering the design effectiveness of controls:

- competence of control owner;
- segregation of conflicting duties;

- independence of source material; and
- past errors that were not prevented or detected in a timely manner.

The control owner should be experienced and trained in such a way that he might be expected to either prevent errors, or, alternatively, having detected errors, be able to appreciate the nature and extent of any corrective action required as a result of their discovery. For example, the bank reconciliation control is only effectively designed where the preparer is able to identify unusual items such as stale cheques or unrecorded bank charges and able to follow up on their remediation by processing the corrective journals in the various ledger accounts.

The control owner should, wherever possible, not be involved with conflicting duties such as reviewing his own work or circumventing the intention of the control. (We will return to this area as part of **Chapter 9** on dealing with the fraud risk assessment process.)

Generally, the design of a control is enhanced when the information used as part of its execution is derived from independent sources, rather than being only internally generated.

Where controls have broken down in the past, an assessment is normally conducted to determine whether this was due to an isolated operator error or whether it is indicative of a flawed design in respect of the control. It may also have been the result of an unexpected event arising for which the design of the control did not allow for.

In the next chapter we will focus on the various techniques that can be used to assess the design effectiveness of controls and strategies.

Potential Risks

We previously discussed that the risk assessment process might also reveal potential risks – those that have not yet crystallised. It is typically not necessary to implement controls for such risks. Instead, management might use the principles of scenario planning to consider what appropriate responses might look like should the potential risks become real. Of course, these hypothetical responses could not be assessed for design and operational effectiveness until such time as they are actually implemented. However, it might provide management with a reasonable blueprint that might quickly be 'pulled from the shelf' in the event of need. By making an investment upfront, it should allow for valuable time and resources to be saved during the critical period shortly after a major new, but expected, risk has crystallised. (As the same principles would be applicable, we will discuss this concept further as part of **Chapter 8** on disaster recovery.)

Updating Risk

As mentioned above, the risk management process should normally be conducted for, and completed as at, a specific point in time.

Wrap-up

It is important that the process reaches a definitive conclusion at a certain stage so as to establish a fixed benchmark or reference point against which to compare both the original expectations and any subsequent developments.

Occasionally, the department tasked with the risk management implementation might struggle to reach such a definitive conclusion for a specific business unit because new information is continuously becoming available. For the process to be effective, however, a report date should be determined and explicitly stated. Any subsequent developments or remediation should then be captured in a future report. The report date would usually be within a couple of days after the last interview with management. The intervening days would be used to collate and document the information in the risk report so that it can be shared with local management for their review. Depending on the thoroughness of the original interviews, the review by local management should be limited to typographical changes or, at most, minor edits. In such a scenario, it would generally not be necessary to re-date the risk report to reflect the date that local management actually agreed to its issuance.

Local management might, on the other hand, require such extensive revisions to the draft risk report that the final version of its wording cannot be agreed between the parties. In order that the issuance of the risk report is then not endlessly deferred, the risk management department should consider whether to issue the report together with a clear indication of the areas where the disagreement still exists. The verbatim responses from local management might also be included to allow the board to conclude on the reasonability of the various versions. It is important for the robustness of the process that local management and the risk management department feel that their comments are given due regard by the board of directors.

Even in circumstances where there are no disagreements, significant delays between the report date and the date of final issuance can undermine the usefulness of the risk report. Every effort should, therefore, be made by the risk management department to resolve all open questions associated with the risk report of one business unit before proceeding to the next business unit. Where staff members conduct interviews and prepare the draft report, the review by the risk department manager should normally occur while his team is still in the field at that business unit. It might otherwise be logistically difficult for the team to return to a business unit to request additional information once they have withdrawn from the field or moved to the next business unit. Local management would also have moved on to other areas and might no longer have the time commitments to extensively revisit the process.

Embedding the Process

Depending on its size and the resources available, an organisation should generally aim to complete the implementation of risk assessments for all in-scope business within one year (and preferably within the same financial year). This is to allow a reasonable aggregation and comparison of all the business units with reference to, broadly speaking, a single point in time.

Where this is not possible, the board should be cognisant of the fact that direct comparisons between various business units might no longer be reasonable, as the overall socio-economic environment in which they operate might have significantly changed during the period.

An organisation with limited risk management resources might then consider a number of alternative implementation plans:

- risk assessments by divisions;
- shortened re-assessment timeline; or
- delegation of re-assessment process.

The **'by division' approach** aims to complete risk assessments for all business units that fall within a specific division in the timeframe of the financial year. As we saw in an earlier example, an organisation has multiple business units (across various jurisdictions) in its manufacturing division as well as other business units in its servicing and maintenance divisions. The board might determine to focus the resources of the risk management department to complete the manufacturing division (and its divisional head office) first, before moving on to the other divisions. The risk assessment at the corporate head office, due to its strategic importance of oversight, should typically also be completed for each of the divisional assessments. In this way, large multi-layer organisations might be broken down into smaller, more manageable segments.

As an alternative, the board might accept that during the first implementation of the risk management programme, the process could extend beyond a single year. They might then determine that the re-assessment programme (during which each business unit is re-visited and its risk assessment updated) be conducted on an annual timeline. The issue of comparing business units operating in potentially different risk environments is therefore avoided in the years beyond the initial implementation.

A combination of the above approaches is where once the risk department has completed its assessments at a specific division, the process is then delegated to its local management to maintain. This would allow the risk management department to focus on the other divisions or newly acquired businesses. Where the process have been delegated, local management would still be required to do an annual re-assessment together with preparing (or updating) the previous risk report. The process as a whole should still be consistent across these business units as each local management team would retain the same template and approach from what was implemented by the risk management department. To ensure the continued robustness of the process, the risk management department might select a couple of these business units, either randomly or on a rotational basis, for which to review their re-assessments.

Re-assessment Process

The risk items facing the various business units, and the organisation as a whole, are continuously evolving and so are the likelihood and impact of their occurrences. The risk management process should similarly be a continuous process.

Once the implementation process has been completed, the re-assessment process should be formally conducted on at least an annual basis.

The re-assessment process essentially involves all the same steps as the original implementation. It is expected, however, that the re-assessment process would be much quicker, as the risk register, risk map and previous risk report have already been completed. The purpose of the re-assessment process is as follow:

- identification of new risks;
- confirmation of consistency of responses;
- follow-up on remediation plans; and
- revision to the risk map.

Although the majority of the risks identified during the original implementation would still be relevant during the subsequent re-assessments, a small number of new risks might emerge (or some risks might have disappeared). It is important that these new risks be identified, graded, accepted, aggregated and controlled in the same consistent manner as the original risks. In the updated risk report to the board of directors these new risks (along with the risks that disappeared) should be highlighted for their attention and consideration.

Similarly, the responses to existing risks might have changed from the original implementation. Local management would have been able to monitor the effectiveness of their initial strategies during the intervening period and determined whether they are still adequate in mitigating the associated risk items. Revisions to these strategies and controls would then also require new assessments of their design and operating effectiveness. The attention of the board should be drawn to changes in the controls and strategies. Where the original control owner has been replaced with a new employee it would, generally, not require a full re-assessment of design effectiveness, provided that the replacement is of similar experience, competence and seniority. Consideration should, however, be given to whether potentially conflicting duties are still appropriately segregated where internal re-organisations took place.

The initial risk assessment might have generated a number of recommendations for local management to improve the control environment. During the re-assessment, the progress made in adopting these recommendations should be tracked and included in the updated risk report. The board would typically expect to see a 'churn' rate in respect of these recommendations. Put another way, local management should be expected to adopt a high percentage of the recommendations during the period between the risk reports.

The location of the risk items on the risk map would also be expected to change over time as more information becomes available. This would then feed into the overall risk map as part of the aggregation phase of the re-assessment process.

Conclusion

In this chapter we discussed the various phases of the risk management process. In the next chapter we will now consider various aspects of the allocation and monitoring of controls.

Chapter 7

Verifying Controls and Strategies

Introduction

In the previous chapter we discussed the various phases of the risk management process in general and controlling risk in particular. In this chapter we will focus in more detail on the various aspects of controls and strategies.

Allocating Controls

We previously discussed that the board of directors can determine to allocate controls to various levels of management throughout the organisation. The basic premise is that the more significant a risk is to the organisation as a whole, the higher level of oversight is required. The aggregated group risk map provides a useful starting point for the board to make this allocation.

'Green Sector' Risk Items

Inherent risks items that fall below the diagonal line of the group risk map (in other words that fall within the 'green' (or lightly shaded) sectors of the risk map) would typically be allocated to the local management of the relevant business units.

Local management should have a broad discretion as to the design of the controls implemented in response to these risk items because, in aggregate, they are expected to have a lower likelihood of a significant impact on the organisation as a whole. That is not to say, however, that these risk items might not have a potentially significant impact on the individual business units themselves.

Depending on the nature of the organisation as a whole, green sector items usually fall within the 'human resources, operational and financial reporting' areas.

'Amber Sector' Risks

The inherent risk items that fall around the diagonal line on the risk map typically require some involvement from management at the corporate head office and, occasionally, the board of directors. These risks would normally fall into the 'legal', 'strategic' and 'hybrid' categories.

'Red Sector' Risks

Effective responses to the inherent risk items that fall above the diagonal line on the risk map usually require the involvement of management at, a minimum, the corporate head office or often board of directors level. These risks would normally be from the 'external' category and some from the 'hybrid' and 'strategic' categories of risk, as discussed in **Chapter 6**.

The board also needs to review the aggregated residual group risk map to assess whether too much management oversight and control have potentially been allocated to certain risk items. Where an overwhelming majority of the risk items have dropped below the diagonal line on the residual risk map, it might indicate that the organisation is strongly risk averse or that lower risk items are unnecessarily escalated to too-high levels within the organisation. Although an extensive escalation policy might reduce the level of residual risk, it needs to be weighed against the opportunity cost associated with senior management and the board of directors getting involved in the responses to relatively minor risks.

Tracking Strategies

As alluded to in **Chapter 6**, notwithstanding the fact that certain strategies can commandeer significant proportions of the resources of the organisation, the actual effectiveness of such strategies is not necessarily easily verified and tested.

The following broad criteria are, however, useful in assessing and keeping track of the results of any strategy:

- the ultimate goal or objective of the strategy;
- the individual milestones in achieving the objective;
- budgets for resource allocations; and
- overall sponsor, project manager and individual owners.

Setting Overall Goals

It is important that a specific, quantifiable objective or goal is established for each strategy. For example, as a response to risk in respect of the **global and domestic recessions** (being the risk classified as **'E1'** in accordance with the naming convention used in **Chapter 6**), the organisation determines to merge a number of currently separate businesses to realise economies of scale. The goal can then be set as follows:

> "Grow the combined profit before tax value of these affected businesses by 50% over the next five years."

This primary goal might also be further developed into a number of secondary objectives which each contribute, in combination, to achieving the overall goal. For example, one of the secondary objectives might be to reduce the overhead costs by 20% over the five years, while another might be to grow the gross margin or contribution by the percentage needed to align with the primary goal. In certain cases, tertiary goals might even be needed in support of the secondary goals. For example, the percentage growth expected to come from sales volumes as opposed to growth from pricing.

The primary goal needs to be analysed or cascaded out in this way because the actual steps and plans required to achieve each of the secondary and tertiary goals would necessarily be different. It also ensures that a complex strategy is broken down into manageable parts that can be assigned to specific owners or responsible parties. The board of directors, when reviewing the design effectiveness of the strategy, should not only consider whether the goals are realistic, but also ensure that they are not in conflict with one another, or in fact mutually exclusive.

In response to each secondary (or tertiary) goal, a separate plan should be developed. For example, the goal of overhead cost reduction might be achieved by migrating all the back office functionality of those separate business units into a single shared service centre. Another plan might be to put the existing service contracts or supply agreements with third parties out to tender as a combined entity in order to secure volume discounts.

Individual Milestones

Depending on the complexity or duration of a specific plan, separate milestones might be required. For example, the migration to the shared service centre (see above) would most likely require the following discreet work streams that might be managed and completed either in parallel with each other or sequentially, depending on their nature:

EXAMPLE: WORK STREAMS REQUIRED TO ESTABLISH A SHARED SERVICE CENTRE

- Documentation of the current practices and processes at each of the affected business units
- Determination of the intended best practices and procedures at the shared service centre
- Calculation of the expected transactional throughput volumes based on plans to achieve the other secondary goals (such as margin growth)
- Mapping of the existing roles and approval matrices at the various business units to the new shared services organisational chart
- Benchmarking of the shared services structure and headcount to ensure the realisation of the procedural enhancements and productivity improvements
- Development of key performance indicators (such as tracking the occurrence of 'stock-outs' or the frequency of order entry errors) to track the effectiveness of the shared service centre
- Cataloguing of the pre-migration level of support provided by the various back-offices to their front-offices
- Migration from the multiple existing IT platforms and applications to a single IT instance and chart of accounts
- Assessment of the physical requirements, such as the floor space of the combined warehouse and administration offices
- Consideration of any regulatory or tax implications of collapsing the existing legal structures of the business units into a single entity
- Outlining the responses to the human resource implications associated with the rationalisation of the existing roles and responsibilities at the business units
- Calculation of the potential impact on the financial reporting of the combined entity from the harmonization of the accounting policies across the business units.

The milestones should be documented together with the detailed steps needed to complete each of them. The expected completion dates of these milestones should also be mapped out on a project calendar.

Budgets

Another method to ensure that progress is being made towards realising the overall strategy is to keep track of the actual funds incurred as well as those still likely to be spent by means of a budget. Although it might be difficult to estimate the exact total expenditure required at the outset of a strategy, it is nevertheless important that, at a minimum, broad outlines of costs are determined. Where possible, these costs should be supported by independent quotes or detailed calculations, rather than 'round number guesstimates'. For example, the costs associated with the migration to a single IT platform should be calculated based on third-party tender responses received, rather than the rounded down costs of maintaining the existing IT applications. That said, organisations prudently include a contingency reserve calculated as a percentage of the overall cost estimate to account for any unforeseen expenditure.

The expected benefits flowing from the strategy should typically not be assumed as 'round numbers' either. Often, strategies expect 'efficiency gains' or the 'elimination of waste' to generate a large portion of the benefits without necessarily determining how these would be achieved. In **Chapter 3**, we discussed how risk management is primarily focused on removing the downside of uncertainty rather than enhancing the upside of over-achievement on the strategy. Similarly, unexpected benefits might very well be realised from the successful strategy, but these should generally not be included in a budget that is to be used as a project management tool. This treatment is consistent with the accounting philosophy that costs are recorded as soon as they become likely, but that profits are only booked when they are actually achieved.

Where the strategy is expected to be rolled out over a number of years, or the expected benefits will only be realised in the periods subsequent to the incurring of the costs, a **discounted cash flow** model should be used. This is to account for the time-value of money as well as to reflect the risk or uncertainty inherent in any projection of future benefits.

The discount rate to be used can be calculated with reference to the weighted average cost of capital of the organisation as a whole, adjusted by an additional premium to reflect the perceived incremental riskiness associated with the strategy. For example, a strategy of only requiring existing third-party service providers to re-tender across an enlarged entity is likely to be less risky than a full back office integration of the processes and procedures of the constituent business units. Where the net discounted cash flow is positive, the strategy is likely to create value for the organisation in the sense that the benefits are expected to exceed the cost of financing the endeavour.

The board of directors, when assessing whether to proceed with the strategy or not, might, however, also consider the 'headroom' or margin of error associated with that cash flow model. In particular, where the net cash flow is at, or near, break-even, additional consideration ought to be given to determine whether the costs have not been understated or the benefits inflated to manipulate the decision to proceed or not. Usually, the costs are incurred in the early years of the model and the benefits only expected in future years. As a result of the discounting mechanism, changes to the level of costs, especially the upfront ones, would tend to have a much greater impact on the viability of the strategy than overstating the savings in the distant future.

The discounted cash flow should be periodically updated throughout the implementation of the milestones with the actual amounts incurred and realised. A variance analysis to explain the difference between the old estimates and the actual amounts might also provide useful insight to allow the stress-testing of the accuracy and reasonability of the remaining estimates as well as to indicate where remedial action might be required.

The implementation of the strategy might also be structured in such a way that at least some of the cash flows associated with the various individual milestones are independent of each other. This would allow management to evaluate the expected benefits throughout the project on an almost real-time basis, rather than only at its ultimate conclusion. Where the results of the early milestones indicate that the net benefits are significantly below expectation, management could determine to abandon or significantly curtail the remainder of the milestones instead of absorbing additional resources. Such a 'hurdle' approach (whereby the milestones are individually assessed and managed) is, however, not always feasible in a complex strategy with multiple, interlinking parts.

Project Sponsor and Manager

An organisation might appoint a specific project sponsor responsible for each major strategy. We have already discussed in **Chapter 5** the role of such an executive sponsor in the context of the implementation of the enterprise risk management programme in general.

Each of the milestones and, depending on the complexity of the strategy, the detailed work steps should have owners assigned to them who are responsible for ensuring the completion on a timely basis and within the associated budget.

An overall project manager should also be appointed to oversee the day-to-day running of the strategy as well as the assessing and tracking of the progress of implementation. The complete strategy, along with goals, work steps, implementation timelines and budgets, is typically captured in a business case document that might, depending on its significance, be presented to the board of directors or senior group management for approval. In addition, an independent risk assessment of the project might be prepared to ensure that all potential risks and concerns have been captured along with adequate responses.

Following the achievement of the strategy, a post-implementation review is conducted to assess which aspects of the project worked well and where improvements might be required going forward. The templates and methodologies can then be re-used in future strategies and projects.

'Walkthroughs' of Controls

Unlike the guidelines used to track the effectiveness of strategies, as discussed above, the methodologies used for controls are much more established and standardised. The design effectiveness of controls, for example, is generally assessed by performing a 'walkthrough' of the process into which those controls fall. Organisations typically have the following fairly standardised processes:

- order to cash / sales cycle;
- procure to pay / purchases cycle;
- cash management / treasury cycle;

- manufacturing / inventory cycle;
- human resource / payroll cycle; and
- financial reporting / close cycle.

These broad processes might be further specified into specific sub-processes. For example, in the **order to cash cycle**, the following sub-processes are normally present:

- customer setup, including creditworthiness assessment;
- processing of customer orders;
- delivery of goods or performance of service;
- invoicing and revenue recognition;
- debt collection and receipting of cash;
- returns and issuance of credit notes; and
- assessment of doubt debt provision.

Within the standard process and sub-processes, the actual controls or procedures might, of course, vary significantly based on the size, complexity or sophistication of each of the business units. For example, credit checking might range from involving, say, a separate department (or credit committee) that utilises proprietary data analysis techniques at one extreme of the scale to a credit controller informally reviewing the potential customer's latest published set of accounts at the other end of the scale.

A walkthrough of a process involves selecting a recent transaction or activity and following it through each of the stages from its initiation to its processing, execution and eventually to its recording in the financial statements.

For example, a sales order in a previous month from **Customer A** might be used for the order to cash cycle, the sub-processes for which are as set out above. The credit controller that reviewed the most recent credit limits of Customer A should be interviewed to determine the level of due diligence that was undertaken prior to giving his approval. Other documentary evidence, such as the completion of the credit assessment template and latest published accounts of Customer A, might also be inspected for internal consistency.

The original sales order from Customer A should then be compared to the picking slip, generated for the warehouse staff to fill the order, to ensure accuracy and timely execution. It should then be traced through to the dispatch docket or proof of delivery to ensure that the invoice was correctly generated and the associated revenue recognized in the appropriate accounting period.

The debtors listing should be inspected to verify that the invoice was being aged in accordance with the sales terms prior to settlement. The remittance advice received from Customer A should then be traced back to the receipting procedures to ensure that cash application has been correctly performed. Where payment has not yet been received, enquiries should be made from the collections clerk to determine the reasonableness of the measures taken and the likelihood of success. This might also, where relevant, feed into the discussions with the credit controller/finance manager in respect of any bad debt provisioning.

It is unlikely that any single transaction would necessarily touch on all key controls. In the example above, Customer A did not return any of the goods or dispute the invoice, and there was, therefore, no need to process a credit note. In such a scenario, the specific 'returns and credit note' sub-process might be walked through separately by selecting a recent relevant transaction.

Similarly, the interviews and enquiries of the control owners might be expanded (beyond the specific transaction selected for the walkthrough) to include discussions on any past examples of where an error was detected and the nature of the remediation steps then undertaken.

The **overall purpose of the walkthrough** is therefore as follows:

- document and understand the flow of information and transactions in the process;
- identify significant points in the sub-processes along with their associated key controls;
- identify any missing or inappropriately designed key controls;
- ascertain the competence and experience of the owners of the key controls; and
- identify conflicting duties or incompatible responsibilities in the process.

It is important that the process is documented as part of the walkthrough and that the transactions selected are clearly identified such that the process can be repeated by an independent person as required. The names and job titles of those interviewed should also be documented.

Walkthroughs would also generate the information needed to compare and contrast processes across different business units. This might be particularly useful in support of a strategy to integrate back office functionality as described earlier in this chapter. By analysing the existing processes for various business units, an ideal or model process could be distilled. This would necessarily mean that the controls in certain processes would need to be improved, but that other controls might be toned down. In particular, the frequency of when a control operates, as well as the level or seniority of the control owner, might be streamlined. It is not necessarily appropriate or efficient that, as a result of any back office integration, the new model processes reflect only that of the most controlled business units (also known as 'a race to the top').

Although a walkthrough does not provide any assurance that the controls have operated for an entire period, it does allow an experienced risk manager or internal auditor to conclude on the design effectiveness of the process in general and the specific controls in particular. Put another way, the reviewer can, based on the result of the walkthrough, conclude that if those controls actually operate as described that they would be effective to prevent or detect significant errors.

Monitoring of Controls

A key component in the risk management process is the continuous monitoring or verification of whether the controls and strategies have actually operated as intended in their design. The board of directors might determine to use any of the following methods, either individually or in conjunction with one another, to verify this compliance:

- certifications;
- questionnaires;
- self-assessments;
- site visits from the risk management department; and
- internal audit department.

Certifications

This is the least intrusive method for monitoring the operational effectiveness of controls. In essence, it exclusively relies on the competence, independence and professionalism of the local management at each of the business units to review their own work. The risk management department or function would typically circulate a standardised template to the local management teams containing a statement to the effect that the undersigned confirm that all the controls have operated in accordance with their design and for the period under review. The template might also provide for local management to respond with any exceptions that were noted and how these were remediated.

The risk management department or function would then normally only collate the responses and summarise any trends for the board of directors.

With this approach, it is completely down to the discretion of local management as to the extent of due diligence they wish to embark upon in advance of certifying compliance. It would generally be expected though that the senior managers would require a similar certification from their middle managers, and so forth down the command chain, prior to signing off the declaration to the corporate head office and the board.

Questionnaires

Similar to the approach discussed in **Chapter 6** of issuing questionnaires to local management as part of the identifying risk phase, questionnaires can also be used to monitor compliance. That list is normally extended to include specific questions on whether local management became aware of any breakdowns of controls during the period under review and how these were dealt with. It is more structured than the certification process, as the questionnaire could be drafted as a checklist against which to compare the actions of local management. For example, questions on the control over stock counts might be set out as follows:

> **EXAMPLE: QUESTIONS REGARDING CONTROL OVER STOCK COUNTS**
>
> - Was at least one full stock completed within the period under review?
> - Did the count teams consist of two individuals?

> - Were the quantities per the system blanked-out for all stock items to be counted?
> - Were variances, in isolation or in aggregate, in excess of €1,000 identified?
> - Were these variances investigated and the stock items recounted were appropriate?
> - Were the quantities per the system updated to reflect the actual number counted?

The list of questions might need to be extensive in order to anticipate the various eventualities associated with distinct business units. It might, therefore, make the timely completion of the questionnaire administratively burdensome. In addition, some of the questions might be ambiguous or subject to individual interpretation. That said, the approach may be well suited for organisations with a decentralised, established structure and a small corporate head office function. The approach is again dependent on the quality and commitment from local management to complete the questionnaires in an honest and transparent manner.

The risk management department would normally enter the results into a spreadsheet model that could extract trends for the board. For example, the number of business units that identified significant variances from their stock count in the current year compared to the prior year.

Self-assessments

This approach is broadly the same as certification, with the notable exception that the level of due diligence required from local management is directed from the corporate head office. For example, the risk management department would instruct local management as to the nature and extent of testing the performance of their controls, with specific guidance on sample selections, methods of testing and treatment of exceptions. The guidance would usually be more 'principles'-based than the 'rules'-based approach of the questionnaires described above. The certification template might also include an additional statement along the lines of a confirmation that the required verification procedures were performed to support the overall certification of control effectiveness.

The risk management department might also, on a rotational basis, review whether the test work performed by local management is in accordance with the guidance issued. Where it is found that local management have not complied with the guidance, or that the results of the test work do not support the overall certification, the applicable business unit might be subjected to independent testing for a number of future periods.

Risk Management Department

The risk management department or function might monitor compliance through their detailed follow-up interviews with local management of each business unit. This would normally take the form of the verbal completion of the questionnaires described above. The major benefit of this verification method is that the interviewer should be able to hone in on specific areas of concern and skip over the items that are not applicable. The risk management department would be responsible for the administration associated with the completion of the questionnaire. While this should reduce the burden on local management, the risk management department would need to be sufficiently resourced to allow for period visits at all the business units across the organisation during an annual cycle.

Internal Audit

An internal audit department is usually well-equipped to develop and then execute test programmes to monitor compliance in general. Although, traditionally, many of the test programmes would have been drafted with reference to financial integrity risks, these scripts should be robust enough to be expanded to cover all controls.

This is the most intrusive of the verification methods, but also provides the most comfort that the controls actually operated as intended and for the period expected.

The nature and extent of the testing is determined by the frequency at which the controls operate. For example, the number of items selected for testing might be as follows:

Example: Suggested Sample Size

Control	Frequency	Sample size
Three-way matching of purchases	Daily	25 – 30
Bank reconciliations of all trading accounts	Weekly	5 – 10
Creditor reconciliation to supplier statement	Monthly	2 – 3
Stock count	Quarterly	2
Computation of corporation tax charge and accrual	Annually	1

If the tester identifies an error from the sample selected, he has an option to extend the population to determine whether the error was an isolated incident or indicative that the control did not operate as intended for the whole period under review. Local management normally have to remediate controls that have failed, after which internal audit can retest another sample to determine its effectiveness.

Samples are required to be selected in an unbiased manner, which usually means randomly rather than haphazardly. This also allows the results to be statistically extrapolated on the entire population of the control and provide the necessary support to reach an overall conclusion on its operating effectiveness.

The nature of the actual test work includes the following:

- inspection;
- enquiries; and
- re-performance.

Inspection is generally the review of the documentary proof that the control operated. For example, the tester would inspect a request for payment for evidence of review (such as tick marks or explanatory notes) as well as the sign-off from the reviewer.

The tester might also make **enquiries** of the control owner to understand what that person checked as part of their review and how any exceptions or questions were resolved.

Finally, the tester might **re-perform** some or all of the checks the control owner made as part of the control to verify whether a similar conclusion could be reached. For example, in a bank reconciliation, the amounts might be vouched back to the supporting documentation such as the bank statement and the general ledger balance.

It is generally not necessary or efficient that a tester performs all three types of tests for each control. The tester would, instead, vary the nature of his testing across all the controls. He might also adopt a rotational testing strategy whereby a specific control that was verified through enquiry is re-performed the following year.

The testing is normally scheduled in the third or fourth quarters of the financial year to ensure that the majority of the controls have sufficiently operated to allow for a valid sample to be selected. It also allows time for local management to remediate any failed controls well in advance of the year-end. Where an insufficient population exists from which to draw the sample or where the testing was conducted in the first half of the financial year, additional or 'top-up' procedures might be required closer to the year-end.

The internal audit department would prepare a report for each business unit tested that sets out the scope and nature of testing along with the results and remediation required. The risk management department would usually review and summarise the individual reports for presentation to the board of directors.

Reliance on the Work of Others

External auditors, as part of their statutory audit of financial statements, typically aim, where possible, to rely on controls to reduce the nature, extent and timing of their substantive procedures. The risk management department should, therefore, liaise and coordinate with the external auditors to determine the best way to leverage this potential overlap.

In particular, the external auditors are required to perform a risk assessment as part of the planning phase of the audit. Although the output from the enterprise risk management programme would cover a much broader area than that of the statutory audit, the risks identified, in particular the ones around financial integrity, should also inform the external auditors.

Audit standards require external auditors to perform walkthroughs of the significant processes used by the entity in the production of the amounts in the financial statement. The walkthroughs outlined above should, therefore, be conducted in such a manner that the external auditors, based on their internal methodologies, might make maximum use of. This could mean that the walkthroughs are conducted under the direct supervision of the external auditors, on their templates and using their documentation protocols. At the same time, this should assist the risk management department to conclude on the design effectiveness of the associated controls for their own purposes.

The external audit plan might also seek to adopt a 'control-based' approach, whereby reliance is placed on the operating effectiveness of internal controls. The external auditors would need to be satisfied with the competence and independence of the testers, which would normally mandate the involvement from either an in-house or outsourced internal audit department. The sample sizes, selection methodologies and the nature of the test procedures would also need to be agreed with the external auditors in advance of the commencement of fieldwork. The output from the monitoring of control effectiveness would then be of benefit to the external audit as well as the internal enterprise risk management programme.

Conclusion

In this chapter we have discussed various aspects of the verification of the operating effectiveness of controls and strategies and how these might be aligned to the requirement from external auditors in respect of the statutory audit process. In the next chapter, we will focus on the specific controls and strategies an organisation might adopt as part of its disaster recovery programme.

Chapter 8

Disaster Recovery

Introduction

In the previous chapters we discussed the various phases of a typical risk management programme. In this chapter we will focus on the specific responses that an organisation can adopt to mitigate risk in respect of **business continuity or disaster recovery** (being the risk classified as **'O2'** in accordance with the naming convention used in **Chapter 6** above).

'Disaster recovery' is the encompassing catalogue of responses by an organisation to catastrophic, unexpected and potentially destructive events. Such events, by their nature, are outside the control of management. They also tend to fall outside the normal business operations of the organisation due to their significance, pervasiveness or uniqueness. Examples of such events may include:

- 'Acts of God' such as earthquakes, flooding or severe cold weather;
- terrorism or malicious destruction;
- infectious disease; and
- information technology failure.

Whereas each of these events, in and of itself, may result in the failure of the organisation as a whole, they tend to affect different areas of the business. For example:

- facilities – such as manufacturing plants and warehouses;
- information technology – such as servers and databases;
- human resources – incapacity of key decision makers; or
- administration – such as head offices and shared service centres.

The responses to the various potential disasters also tend to be different, driven by the areas of the organisation affected. We will consider examples of these responses later in the chapter.

Disaster Recovery Plan

Whether a disaster occurs or not is typically outside of the control of management. Nevertheless, an organisation can devise an appropriate infrastructure, by way of a disaster recovery plan, to deal with the consequences of such as an emergency in advance.

The disaster recovery plan should be maintained in duplicate hard copy format and would typically include the following considerations:

- definition of what constitutes a disaster or emergency;
- names and contact details of all members of the disaster recovery team;
- details of assigned responsibilities of each member of the disaster recovery team;
- primary location of the command centre (along with an alternate location);
- catalogue of key information requirements;
- pre-developed templates for tracking progress in the resolution of the disaster or emergency; and
- pre-proposed action steps to the various anticipated emergency scenarios.

Administration

For a geographically dispersed organisation it might be appropriate to devise separate disaster recovery plans for each significant business unit, because an emergency at one would not necessarily require a complete shutdown of or response from the entire organisation. In addition, the corporate head office would also have a separate disaster recovery plan to cover all the functions and activities performed there.

In the same way as the roll-out and implementation of the risk management programme should be standardised and directed from the corporate head office, so too should the template for planning and designing the disaster recovery plans be provided centrally. Each business unit would then be expected to determine its particular emergencies and their appropriate responses. The central risk management function initially (and the board of directors ultimately) would also review each of the individual plans for completeness and reasonability. The board would generally delegate one of the senior executives as the corporate sponsor for the initiative to ensure adequate involvement from management throughout the organisation.

Each member of the disaster recovery team should retain two copies in hard copy format. One of the copies should be kept at his primary business address or office and the other at a safe alternate location, which is usually his private residence. This is to ensure that the plan is always available, even when the administrative offices are inaccessible.

The plan should be reviewed on an, at least, annual basis to determine whether the information contained therein is still current and whether any additional risks or revised responses have been identified and developed in the interim period since the last review.

A programme should also be developed to train the disaster recovery team in their duties and, to the extent feasible, dry-run testing should be conducted on a regular basis. Certain aspects, such as fire drills and other evacuations, can be tested on a frequent basis. More significant interventions, such as emergency plant closures, can be co-ordinated with normal, scheduled maintenance shut-downs to avoid excessive disruptions.

Activating the Disaster Recovery Plan

It is important to precisely define upfront what is understood to constitute an *emergency*. This would act as a trigger for the disaster recovery plan to be activated and the normal reporting structures and authority levels applicable in the organisation or business unit to be temporarily suspended.

The standardised templates, which would have been developed in anticipation of an emergency, should assist in providing a framework for the disaster recovery team in which to determine the appropriate next action steps. For example, a pre-populated list of employees to allow for the capturing of their whereabouts and to track the dissemination of information is a useful tool to ensure nobody is omitted through oversight.

Disaster Recovery Team

The disaster recovery team is an ad hoc committee specifically designated to assess and resolve an emergency through the execution of the disaster recovery plan. This team would require expertise from across the business unit or organisation as a whole and would typically consist of, at least, the following members:

- team leader;
- administrative support;
- information technology team member;
- facilities team member;
- communications team member; and
- human resource team member.

Each of these team members should also have a nominated alternate that can step into the place of the original team member should he become incapacitated. Organisations with large or complex operations might determine to establish larger teams in, for example, IT, than just an individual member and alternate. The detailed discussion below will assume the creation of such larger teams.

Team Leader

The team leader would normally be a senior manager in the business unit or of the organisation as a whole. His or her responsibilities vis-à-vis the disaster recovery plan are as follows::

- owning, maintaining and distributing the plan;
- ensuring adequate awareness of and training in the execution of the plan;
- declaring the existence of an emergency and thereby suspending the normal organisational structures and authority limits;
- evaluating the nature of the emergency and activating the relevant action steps;
- communicating with senior executives at the corporate head office and any regulatory authorities;
- contacting and briefing emergency services and insurance claims inspectors;
- coordinating the activities of the other disaster recovery team members;

- authorising emergency expenditure; and
- declaring the resolution of the emergency and thereby the re-instatement of the normal organisational structures and authority limits.

The team leader should normally have a personal assistant to provide administrative support such as arranging meetings or to track down the whereabouts of team members. In addition, the personal assistant might be used to purchase miscellaneous supplies and equipment.

Command Centre

The team leader should normally be based in the command centre (or its alternate location) for the duration of the emergency. The command centre should be geographically separate from, although within easy reach of, the main place of business of the organisation. The command centre should also have adequate space and infrastructure (such as tables and chairs) for the whole disaster recovery team to convene on a frequent basis. In addition, the command centre should ideally be equipped with communication equipment such as telephones, computers and internet access.

In order to reduce the cost implications of these redundant systems, a business unit might determine to locate its command centre at the offices of its corporate head office or at one of the other business units, provided that that location is geographically separated and accessible. In that way, a command centre might be 'shared' across multiple business units.

In the unlikely event that the original or primary command centre is also incapacitated by the emergency, an alternative location should be identified. Again, this alternate location can be situated on the premises of another business unit to limit the costs associated with maintenance.

Information Technology Team

As its name suggests the information technology team is primarily responsible for all IT-related matters resulting from the emergency. In particular, the team has the following roles:

- gathering information on the nature and extent of damage to the IT infrastructure;

- coordinating with the offsite data centres to restore the backed-up information;
- testing the accuracy and completeness of the restored information;
- accessing and distributing key information maintained on the IT servers;
- determining the nature, extent and cost of required replacements of the IT infrastructure;
- sourcing and purchasing the replacement IT equipment; and
- configuring the replacement IT equipment to the organisation-specific protocols and security settings.

As part of the normal operating procedures of the IT function at an organisation, transactional data is usually backed-up and stored at off-site locations on a daily basis. The sophistication of these procedures ranges from outsourcing the function to independently audited external service providers at one of the scale and to in-house use of discs and tape drives at the other end. Irrespective of the nature and methodology of the back-ups, it is important that the information so captured is periodically restored and tested to ensure that, in the event of an emergency, the data can in fact be retrieved.

It is also important to ensure the completeness of the information captured. Employees should therefore be instructed not to retain any business data on the hard discs of their laptop and desktop computers. Not only might such information be lost in the event of a hard disc failure, but laptops are also tend to be prone to theft with the resultant potential breaches of information security.

The backup and restore procedures would typically be sufficient to safeguard electronic information. However, organisations might also have made use of extensive paper-based or hard copy information. Such information should, as far as possible, be scanned so that it can also be stored electronically. The original versions of these documents should then be retained in fire-proof safes or at secure locations.

Each member of the IT team should retain two copies (one at their office and the other at a safe alternate location) of the catalogue of the key IT equipment as well as the associated configuration settings. This catalogue should be reviewed and updated, if needed, at least on a quarterly basis.

Facilities Team

The facilities team is generally responsible for all non-IT infrastructures. Specifically their roles include the following:

- gathering information on the nature and extent of damage to the non-IT infrastructure;
- securing or at least restricting access to the damaged facilities;
- assisting emergency services and insurance claims inspectors;
- accessing and distributing key hard-copy only information (that is not maintained on the IT servers);
- determining the nature, extent and cost of replacement plant and non-IT equipment;
- locating appropriate temporary warehouses or administrative buildings; and
- sourcing and purchasing non-IT equipment such as forklifts, desks and physical security systems.

The members of the facilities team would typically require various skill sets, ranging from knowledge of the operations of the warehouse or manufacturing lines to the design layout of the administrative offices. In addition, they are responsible for cataloguing the nature and location of key hard-copy only information that cannot be scanned and saved on the IT servers.

Communications Team

During an emergency the timely communication of information might be of critical importance. Therefore, the disaster recovery team should include a team member whose principal tasks revolve around the effective gathering and dissemination of critical information. In particular the roles of this team include the following:

- maintaining contact, physical addresses and next-of-kin details of all employees;
- maintaining details of key or preferred suppliers and customers;
- disseminating information to all employees;
- drafting official press releases to the media;
- contacting suppliers to re-order raw materials and inventory; and
- contacting key customers in respect of revised delivery timetables.

The purpose of the communication team is to ensure the continuous availability of information to all the internal and external stakeholders of the organisation throughout the duration of the emergency.

Human Resource Team

During an emergency the continued welfare of employees should also be of primary importance. The key roles of the human resource team are therefore as follows:

- verifying the whereabouts of all employees;
- organising counselling and support services to employees where needed;
- activating the succession plans to replace key decision-makers on an interim or permanent basis;
- redrafting the organisational charts to reflect any permanently changed circumstances; and
- assisting in developing and participation in the training programmes for the replacement employees.

Succession plans are usually of a highly sensitive nature and should only be retained by the most senior member (and his alternate) of the team.

Hard copy versions of the other documentation, such as employee contact details, process manuals and organisational charts, should be retained by all members of the team at both their offices and alternate locations.

Scenario Planning

Although emergencies on a scale serious enough to threaten the survival of the organisation are difficult to predict, it might be useful to document proposed responses and action steps in advance to respond to these hypothetical 'what if' scenarios. The actual emergency might, of course, look very different from what was anticipated, but still incorporate at least some aspects from across the various scenarios. The proposed responses might also require amendment based on the severity or exact nature of the disaster. That said, critical time can be wasted by having to start with a 'blank sheet of paper' during an emergency rather than having a previously prepared starting point on which to base the actual action steps.

Effective scenario planning might also reveal weaknesses in normal business processes, such as the absence of a properly maintained list of key suppliers or up-to-date employee contact details. Such information might be useful in the normal course of business and not just during an emergency situation.

Proper disaster recovery requires a level of redundancy and duplication to be built into an otherwise lean process. It is therefore important to also consider as part of the scenario planning whether this excess capacity can be utilised in some efficient manner in order to reduce the associated opportunity costs. We previously indicated that command centres and alternate warehouses or administrative offices might be shared among business units. Alternatively, some employees might be issued with the necessary communication equipment (such as laptops and mobile phone cards) to allow them to perform their work remotely, obviating the need for extensive alternate office space.

Some preventative measures might also be introduced in anticipation of an emergency. For example, an organisation might determine that it is cost effective to immunise its workforce against the annual influenza virus, thereby reducing the likelihood of a significant number of employees falling ill around the same time.

Presented below are some common scenarios along with the proposed responses from the disaster recovery team:

- flooding destroys the warehouse or assembly line;
- a gas explosion forces the evacuation of the administrative offices;
- an outbreak of a highly infectious disease; or
- virus infection or computer hacking of IT servers.

Scenario – Flooding

This scenario has little direct impact on the IT infrastructure or employees of the business unit. It is primarily concerned with a situation that renders the trading or production facilities inaccessible or inoperable. The overall tasks should, therefore, be aimed at limiting the damage to the inventory or equipment and the time delays before normal trading can commence again.

Scenario: Flooding

The detailed actions to be completed by the disaster recovery team would include the following:

- Team leader:
  - Declare an emergency and activate the relevant disaster recovery plan
  - Contact emergency services and insurance inspectors
  - Authorise emergency expenditure
  - Coordinate the activities of the teams and track progress in resolving the emergency.

- Facilities team:
  - Restrict access to the flooded area through physical security measures
  - Confirm with emergency services that premises are safe to be entered and inspected
  - Catalogue the damage to the physical infrastructure and production equipment
  - Assess damage to the inventory held in the warehouse or on the production lines
  - Locate temporary alternate warehouse or production facility
  - Organise the transfer of undamaged inventory and equipment to the alternate location
  - Assist insurance inspectors with the completion of the insurance claims
  - Source replacement equipment either internally (if redundant equipment is available) or externally
  - Determine the appropriate disposal of damaged equipment and inventory
  - Consider feasibility of additional works to safeguard against future flooding

- Human resources team:
  - Establish the whereabouts of all employees

- Communications team:
  - Inform affected employees to remain at home until further notice
  - Re-order replacement inventory and raw materials from list of preferred suppliers
  - Inform key customers of emergency and expected delays in deliveries.

Scenario – Gas Explosion

This scenario is primarily focused on the inability to process back office transactions. Even where there is no structural damage to the administrative offices, the threat of, for example, a gas leak might prevent employees from returning to their offices for an extended period of time. The primary tasks should therefore be aimed at ensuring employee safety and limiting the delays before back office processing can return to normal.

Scenario: Gas Explosion

The detailed actions to be completed by the disaster recovery team would include the following:

- Team leader:
  - Declare an emergency and activate the relevant disaster recovery plan
  - Immediately contact emergency services
  - Authorise emergency expenditure
  - Coordinate the activities of the teams and track progress in resolving the emergency
- Facilities team:
  - Organise the immediate evacuation of all employees to a safe distance from the administrative offices
  - Restrict access to the affected areas through physical security measures

- Turn off the gas supply to the office if it is safe to do so
- Confirm with emergency services when premises are safe to be entered and inspected
- Assess damage to the structural integrity of the building and non-IT equipment such as desks and chairs
- Locate alternate administrative offices where building has been rendered unsafe
- Determine the extent of hard copy information lost and request copies of originals held at off-site locations
- Organise the transfer of all undamaged equipment to the alternate location
- Assist insurance inspectors with the completion of the insurance claims
- Source replacement non-IT equipment either internally (if redundant equipment is available) or externally
- Consider the feasibility of repairing the building or arrange for its demolition

- Information technology team
  - Assess damage to the IT equipment such as servers and desktops
  - Organise with the off-site data centre to restore the most recent backed-up information
  - Determine the extent of electronic information lost
  - Source replacement IT equipment either internally (if redundant equipment is available) or externally
  - Reconfigure replacement IT equipment to in-house communication and security protocols

- Human resources team:
  - Establish the whereabouts of all employees
  - Activate the succession plans where key decision makers have been incapacitated
  - Recruit replacement staff on an interim or permanent basis
  - Assist in training the replacement staff based on the documented process manuals

- Communications team:
  - Contact the next-of-kin of all deceased or injured employees with details of the relevant hospitals
  - Inform employees to return and remain home until further notice
  - Prepare press releases to the media
  - Inform key customers of emergency and expected delays in deliveries.

Scenario – Infectious Disease

This scenario is focussed on a significant number of employees becoming incapacitated over a short period of time. The primary tasks should be to contain the spreading of the infection among the employees and minimise the disruption to front and back office activities. Depending on the severity of the threat, employees might be prevented from returning to work for an extended period of time. In such cases, limited activities might be performed remotely depending on the availability of communication infrastructure and the nature of the work.

SCENARIO – INFECTIOUS DISEASE

The detailed actions to be completed by the disaster recovery team would include the following:

- Team leader
  - Declare an emergency and activate the relevant disaster recovery plan
  - Immediately contact emergency services
  - Authorise emergency expenditure on precautionary measures
  - Coordinate the activities of the teams and track progress in resolving the emergency

- Facilities team
    - Quarantine all affected employees until they can be taken to hospital or return home
    - Confirm with emergency services the appropriate precautionary measures to minimise further contamination
    - Source and distribute or organise these precautionary measures (such as face masks or immunisations) to unaffected employees returning back to work
- Human resources team
    - Establish the whereabouts of all employees
    - Activate the succession plans where key decision-makers have been incapacitated
    - Recruit replacement staff on an interim or permanent basis
    - Assist in training the replacement staff based on the documented process manuals
- Communications team
    - Contact the next-of-kin of all affected employees with details of the relevant hospitals
    - Inform employees to return and remain home until further notice
    - Prepare press releases to the media
    - Inform key customers of emergency and expected delays in deliveries.

Scenario – Computer Virus

This scenario focuses on the IT system being made inoperable through a computer virus or unauthorised access. Even though this might not pose a direct threat to the welfare of the employees or the structural integrity of offices and warehouses, the normal activities of the organisation would be significantly affected. The primary tasks are, therefore, to identify and remove the threat to the computer systems and, where data has been corrupted, to restore the most recent version of the backed-up information.

> **SCENARIO: COMPUTER VIRUS**
>
> The detailed actions to be completed by the disaster recovery team would include the following:
>
> - Team leader
>   - Declare an emergency and activate the relevant disaster recovery plan
>   - Authorise emergency expenditure
>   - Coordinate the activities of the teams and track progress in resolving the emergency
>
> - Information technology team
>   - Assess the nature and details of the threat to the electronic information
>   - Liaise with external service providers on ways to contain and eliminate the threat identified
>   - Perform a full IT system health check to ensure the threat has been removed
>   - Organise with the off-site data centre to restore the most recent unaffected backed-up information
>   - Determine the extent of electronic information lost
>   - Consider the feasibility of enhanced security software and protocols
>   - Assist police in their investigations to identify the perpetrators
>
> - Communications team
>   - Inform employees to suspend processing and e-mailing until further notice
>   - Prepare press releases to the media where personal details of customer have been compromised

Conclusion

In this chapter, we considered the infrastructure needed as well as possible action steps to effectively respond to disasters that impact on the very survival of a business unit or organisation as a whole. In the next chapter, we will focus on specific actions an organisation might consider in response to the pervasive threat of fraud.

Chapter 9

Fraud Considerations

Introduction

In the previous chapters we discussed some suggested infrastructure and responses in respect of disaster recovery at an organisation. In this chapter, we will focus on the infrastructure and responses that an organisation can adopt to mitigate the various risks associated with fraud (being those risks classified as **'F'** risks in accordance with the naming convention used in **Chapter 6** above).

An organisation will usually involve both the corporate head office and the individual business units in its overall response to fraud risks. This is to ensure that a sufficient level of consistency is achieved throughout the organisation by virtue of standardised infrastructure, while at the same time ensuring effective and efficient detailed responses. In this model, the corporate head office would lead the establishment of the required infrastructure such as the fraud policy, reporting mechanisms and risk assessments, whereas the local business units would determine and implement the specific controls best suited to prevent and detect the actual fraudulent actions. In smaller organisations both these activities would typically be performed by a member of the senior management team, such as the finance director. The verification of the efficacy of these responses is rolled into the broader enterprise risk management programme.

By their nature, fraudulent actions are designed to be concealed and it is therefore important that an organisation adopts procedures to try to prevent fraud altogether, rather than focussing solely on methods to detect and resolve suspected frauds.

Definition of Fraud

The basic starting point for any consideration of fraud is to define precisely what is understood by the term 'fraud'. Although it could reasonably be expected that the vast majority of staff would have a general appreciation for what constitutes unacceptable or fraudulent behaviour, management still ought to define such behaviour in a fair amount of detail so as to minimise ambiguity. There is, however, a level of balance required – the more precisely prohibited actions are described, the higher the likelihood that a particular fraud can be designed to specifically circumvent the 'letter' of the policy.

The following broad definition might be used to provide the necessary outline and spirit of any fraud policy:

"Fraud is the intentional falsification of financial information or the unlawful removal of assets to extract value or corruptly gain advantage."

This broad definition can then be further developed, for example to reflect some more specific examples of actions considered to be fraudulent, such as:

- misstatement of financial information through commission (inappropriate capitalisation of expenses) or omission (under accrual of liabilities);
- theft or unauthorised usage of company assets (such as inventory, equipment or cash);
- creation of fictitious supporting documentation (such as authorisations or receipts); or
- corrupt acts (such as bribery).

An organisation might determine to expand upon 'corrupt acts such as bribery' to align its internal definition with that contained in the legislation of the applicable jurisdiction. Where the organisation operates across multiple jurisdictions these definitions might not necessarily be precisely consistent. Organisations should strive to avoid location-specific fraud definitions to avoid situations whereby certain behaviour would be considered fraud in some jurisdictions, but not in others. By allowing such multiple fraud definitions, an organisation raises the risk of an employee exploiting any discrepancies for corrupt advantage. An organisation might, therefore, determine to review the various legal definitions of the jurisdictions in which it operates and draft its own internal definition in accordance with the most restrictive guidance. This is to ensure that its standardised definition would always be in compliance with all the locally applicable laws. To this end, an organisation might require assistance from external legal counsel.

'Tone at the Top'

In order for the fraud definition to 'come alive' throughout the organisation, senior management are required to set the appropriate 'tone at the top' – in essence, sending a clear message that any fraud is viewed in a serious light and that vigorous investigations would invariably be launched and robust action taken where appropriate.

Management have broadly the following mechanisms to set the required tone:

- formal fraud policy;
- reporting mechanisms;
- training programmes;
- certification requirements;
- investigations; and
- fraud risk assessments.

Fraud Policy and Reporting Mechanisms

In **Chapter 4** we indicated that an organisation would generally document its definition of fraud in a specific policy document or as part of a broader code of conduct. Whichever method is chosen, it is important that the definition is easily accessible by all employees through either the circulation of a hard copy version or through electronic access to an intranet site.

The policy document should also outline the mechanisms, as discussed in **Chapter 4**, whereby an instance of suspected fraud would be investigated along with the methods of reporting suspicions of fraudulent behaviour. It is important to include a clear and specific confirmation that no retaliatory actions would be taken against anyone making a bona fide report, so as to encourage employees to share their concerns. It should also serve as a warning to malicious employees that making spurious claims against an innocent party would similarly be viewed as a serious offence, resulting in disciplinary action being taken.

Training Programmes and Certifications

An organisation should strongly consider a training programme to ensure that the written policy is clearly understood and sufficiently known by all of its employees. As part of the induction process all new employees might be presented with a copy of the policy and then automatically enrolled into periodic training sessions that are already scheduled for all the existing employees. Such training sessions would likely need to be repeated a number of times during each financial year to ensure maximum attendance. An organisation might also mandate the attendance at one of these training sessions as part of the performance development programme for each staff member.

A portion of the training session should be devoted to refreshing the principles of the fraud policy. This can be achieved through case studies or hypothetical scenarios that might reasonably confront the audience members on a daily basis. For senior management, on the other hand, a dedicated independent ethics course might be appropriate as their actions are likely to have a more significant impact on the organisation than a single rouge employee.

The training session should also allow for the participants to share ethical dilemmas or questions raised from their own experiences. This would provide valuable feedback to senior management on areas where the existing fraud policy is required to be enhanced or modified. Therefore, the training sessions could be conducted with input and participation from the risk management department or whichever other corporate head office function is tasked with the broader fraud risk management programme.

An organisation might determine that a form of testing at the end of the training session is appropriate to verify the necessary level of knowledge transfer or learning. Employees might then be expected to successfully complete training once every financial year or more frequently in industries possibly more prone to fraud, such as financial services.

An alternative to the formal training and testing approach is a requirement for each employee to certify that they understand and comply with the fraud policy. Again, such certification can be mandated each financial year for all employees, including new hires. This method places the onus on employees to sufficiently familiarise themselves with the principles of the fraud policy and might, therefore, be more aligned to an organisation with such a culture. Employees should, however, still have the necessary access to resources, such as the risk management department, to resolve any questions of interpretation that they might have. The risk management department might similarly publish 'Frequently Asked Questions' or guidance notes to assist employees in this respect.

Investigations

In **Chapter 4**, we discussed the various methods by which investigations might be conducted. It is important that such investigations are, and are seen to be, independent, unbiased and confidential. This would help ensure that an appropriately strong message is sent throughout the organisation that fraud is not tolerated at any level. Employees might become permanently discouraged from raising their concerns about possible fraudulent actions through the reporting mechanisms, where it is perceived that no suitable investigation and actions are taken by senior management. On the other hand, management should take care to respect due process and the presumption of innocence. The human resource department should therefore participate in the drafting of the investigator's terms of reference to ensure compliance with jurisdiction-specific laws and regulations.

Fraud Risk Assessment

An organisation should conduct an, at least bi-annual, formal fraud risk assessment process whereby senior management from across the entire group or company consider the various fraud risks facing the organisation. This process can be seen more as a 'top-down' approach than the normal 'bottom-up' approach adopted for the general enterprise risk management programme. This is because fraud tends to be prevalent across all business units, such that the organisation can benefit from the collective insights of all senior managers. Also, a fraud risk assessment is more anticipatory in nature and therefore management might have to almost act as 'devil's advocates' to tease out the possible risks, rather than deal with responses to existing, known risks.

The steps or phases of the fraud risk assessment are broadly the same as those of the enterprise risk management process described in **Chapter 6**.

Identification of Fraud Risks

For the purposes of the fraud risk assessment, 'senior management' would generally consist of the executive directors, heads of the divisions or business units and representatives from other functions with particular expertise or insights such as the legal and internal audit departments.

The risk management department (or other function tasked with implementing the enterprise risk management programme) would typically facilitate the discussions by preparing a desktop list of possible fraud risks. As a starting point, these fraud risks would usually be related to the detailed definition of fraud. For example, the desktop list of fraud risk might include the following:

- F1 – theft of company assets;
- F2 – improper capitalisation of expenditure;
- F3 – falsification of expense claims;
- F4 – fictitious recording of sales transactions and revenue recognition; and
- F5 – bribery or corrupt acts.

Senior management should then consider whether these and any other risks from their own experiences are generally applicable to the organisation as a whole. Once the broad captions have been identified, management should consider how an employee might go about perpetrating any of these fraudulent actions.

Management should be conscious of the particular circumstances that need to exist to create an appropriate environment for a fraud to occur. In this respect the 'Fraud Triangle' might be a useful tool. At a high-level it requires the following forces to be present:

- Rationalisation;
- Incentive; and
- Opportunity.

'Rationalisation' refers to the internal reasons that an employee uses to justify his actions. For example, the fact that everyone else is doing it, management appear to allow such behaviour or that the organisation 'owes' the employee additional rewards for overtime worked or as a get-even tactic in response to salary cuts.

'Incentive' refers not only to benefits such as monetary or reputational gain, but also the pressure to achieve performance targets or reduce workloads. The fraud might even be designed simply as a way to avoid difficult questions and challenges from analysts or corporate management regarding the performance of the business unit.

'Opportunity' refers to the weakness of the internal controls or the independent oversight, in general, as well as the extent to which conflicting duties are properly segregated.

It is likely that the current recessionary environment would have greatly increased some or all of these forces. In particular, where salary levels have been reduced, certain employees might find it easier to rationalise defrauding their employer to make up for the shortfalls. Similarly, performance targets might be significantly more difficult to achieve in a contracting market, resulting in a threatened reduction in bonus or commission-related compensation. Senior management might also feel obliged to misrepresent the financial position of the organisation to comply with debt covenants and thereby secure continued financial support from the banks. In general, the opportunity for fraud would have increased as well, especially where staff numbers have been significantly reduced, which impacts on the levels of oversight and segregation of duties. Management focus would perhaps also have shifted from detailed oversight to survival planning.

We will consider appropriate strategies and controls in response to these forces later in this chapter. The recession necessarily impacts differently on each organisation. It does, however, underline the need for a frequent and formalised consideration of fraud risks.

Based on the interaction of the above forces, management might determine to describe in more detail the exact scenarios when each of these fraud risks might be perpetrated. For example:

- F1.1 – theft of inventory from warehouse;
- F1.2 – theft of inventory from delivery vehicles;
- F1.3 – theft of cash from premises;
- F5.1 – corrupt payments made to influence government officials;
- F5.2 – gifts received by employees to secure the awarding of sub-contracting arrangements.

Analysing the broader fraud risks into these more specific instances allows for their responses to be more effectively and efficiently crafted.

Grading of Fraud Risks

Not all these detailed fraud risks might necessarily be equally applicable to all the business units of the organisation or indeed equally significant to the organisation as a whole. An inherent risk map is therefore prepared to assist management in grading the importance or significance of each of the fraud risk items.

The nature of the fraud risks might most likely change over time or their prevalence might be affected by changes in the external economic environment. In line with the comments made in respect of the impact of a recessionary environment on fraud, it would generally be expected that the fraud items on the inherent risk map would have drifted diagonally upwards towards the red (or heavily shaded) sectors over the recent past.

Accepting Fraud Risks

Unfortunately, it is not necessarily within management's gift to accept or avoid fraud risks, except perhaps to the extent of not having, say, a petty cash float on the premises at all. We can therefore skip over this phase of the enterprise risk management programme as it is not relevant for the fraud risk assessment process.

Controlling Fraud Risks

Management can introduce a wide variety of strategies and controls to deal with the common fraud risks:

Financial Statement Frauds These frauds relate to risk '**F2 – improper capitalisation of expenditure**' and risk '**F4 – fictitious recording of sales transactions and revenue recognition**'. It is essential that the accounting policies are clearly documented and that the finance community receive proper and continuous training in their application. The internal audit department is also typically well-placed to verify compliance with the policies through inspection of documentation and re-performance of selected transactions. It is important to note that the procedures performed by external statutory auditors are not necessarily designed with the intention of identifying frauds. Organisations need to develop their own internal mechanisms for preventing and detecting fraud, rather than rely on a potential by-product of the annual statutory audit.

Misappropriation Frauds These frauds relate to risk '**F1 – theft of company assets**'. Strong physical security at the various access points to the premises should act as a reasonable deterrent. This would include the use of electronic access cards, security cameras and roving on-site personnel. Frequent or even unscheduled fixed asset verification techniques, such as physically checking the location of laptops and the mileage on company vehicles should also detect and help prevent misuse.

Falsification frauds These frauds relate to risk '**F3 – falsification of expense claims**' and other manipulation of supporting documentation. The authority matrix should clearly outline at what monetary level additional approval is required prior to reimbursing employee expenses. At a minimum, all employees' expenses should be supported by original receipts and be subjected to at least one level of oversight – no employee should be able to 'self-certify' that an expense was incurred. The internal audit department or payroll department might also be utilised to verify whether the nature of the expenses incurred are in line with the documented guidelines of the organisation.

The creation of fictitious vendors might be prevented through the proper segregation of conflicting duties. For example, the employee responsible for creating a new vendor account should neither be allowed to process the receipt of goods and services nor to authorise any payments.

Employees might also be rotated across the various business processes of, say, the finance department. This helps to ensure business continuity in case of the departure or illness of an employee. It also has the added benefit of preventing collusion between two employees to circumvent existing controls. (Some organisations, for example, insist on all their staff taking their holidays through the year, rather than allowing individuals to carry days forward indefinitely, to ensure that roles and activities are rotated periodically between various staff members.)

Corruption In response to corruption, the organisation might have to depend on the controls around the reimbursement of expenses as a means of preventing the payment of bribes to third parties. In respect of detecting whether employees have received bribes in order to award contracts, the organisation might need to rely on confidential tip-offs through hotlines, for example, from colleagues who have noticed changes in lifestyles or expenditure inconsistent with salary levels of their colleagues. Organisations typically document a gift policy that either prohibits the receiving of gifts by its employees altogether or requires such benefits to be at least declared in a register, or even raffled among all the employees of the organisation. Senior management should also ensure that the awarding of large contracts are not necessarily down to a single individual, but rather down to a selection panel through an open tendering mechanism. The panel would then be required to document its reasons for selecting a particular tender proposal by rating each supplier against a pre-established set of criteria. Bonus calculations should be structured in such a manner that their payments are not solely dependent on achieving monetary targets, but should instead be in reference to a balanced scorecard of achieving a number of pre-agreed goals and objectives.

Allocating Controls

We have already discussed how the responsibility for controlling risk should be allocated to that part of the organisation best placed to effectively and efficiently manage it. This implies that fraud risk items that fall in the red sectors of the inherent risk map ought to be subjected to the highest level of oversight, whereas green sector risk items might fall exclusively within the responsibility of local management. Because fraud risks are, however, pervasive and potentially ever-present, the required level of oversight can be an extensive drain on time and management resources. Therefore, an organisation might determine to make the following allocation to achieve an appropriate balance between efficacy and efficiency:

Board of Directors The audit committee (or the board of directors generally) should be responsible for approving the overall fraud policy, the implementation of the associated reporting mechanisms, as well as reviewing all investigation reports flowing from alleged breaches. It should also review the summaries of the bi-annual fraud risk assessments and challenge senior management on their completeness and the adequacy of proposed responses. On a more detailed level, the board, in general, or the chairman, in particular, might review and approve the expense claims from the managing director or other executive directors.

Corporate Management The executive directors and other senior management at the corporate head office would primarily be responsible for providing a second level of review and ensuring consistency of approach across the various business units. For example, the expenses claimed by the divisional management might be reviewed by the group managing director for compliance with the group policies on gifts and travel. The group finance director might also review the assumptions and discount rates used by the business units in calculating, for example, their pension assumptions and goodwill impairments. The risk management department might similarly be tasked to benchmark these assumptions against publically available information from industry peers.

The group controller and his staff might be utilised to review specific or unusual transactions to ensure that the correct accounting treatment was applied. The internal audit department is typically responsible for ensuring that the group policies were consistently applied during the year. Their random site visits might serve as a strong deterrent to unauthorised transactions such as accelerated revenue recognition and inappropriate capitalisation of expenditure.

Business Unit Management Local management would normally be responsible for those frauds that, in a group context, could be considered to be at a less-than-significant monetary level. For example, the theft of petty cash or inventory. Management might determine the most appropriate mechanisms for discouraging such activities that are best suited to their specific business unit. The central internal audit department might then prepare independent reports on the effectiveness of these mechanisms in order to establish a database of best practices.

Segregation of Duties An effective way to design any process to reasonably prevent a fraud is to ensure a proper segregation of conflicting duties. As a broad principle, no single individual should be able to process transactions or make payments without the input or oversight from another employee, who is, at a minimum, on the same level of seniority. Taking that principle all the way to the top of the organisation, the Combined Code requires that the roles of chairman and managing director be performed by separate individuals.

This principle also underlies most of the strategies and controls described above. For example, any non-standard journals should be authorised by a member of senior management, who in turn should not be able to process the actual entry into the general ledger. This is to prevent, e.g. the accountant from attempting to conceal another fraud through the misuse of a manual journal. On the other hand, the finance director, say, should similarly be prevented from unilaterally recording a journal to capitalise expenses. There is, however, a pervasive risk that a senior manager might put undue pressure on a subordinate to process an inappropriate journal. It is therefore necessary that manual journals are retained and reviewed by independent staff such as the internal audit department. Most IT system applications can record all manual journals along with who authorised them and when they were processed. A standard step in an internal audit work plan would then be to analyse the listing of journals for unusual amounts, accounts or those performed outside of normal business hours.

As mentioned above, a single employee should not be able to create or amend vendors as well as authorise payments. This might be a particular challenge in small organisations with limited back office staff. In such cases, the focus should then be on the proper review of supporting documentation prior to the authorisation of the payment. At a minimum, two signatories should be required for all payments. An organisation might develop an approval matrix whereby larger amounts require authorisation from more senior management, sometimes above the business unit itself at the corporate head office level.

To fully determine whether potentially conflicting duties are being performed by the same individual, it is normally necessary to perform a 'walkthrough' of the business process. In **Chapter 7,** we discussed the nature of these walkthroughs as a means to assess the design effectiveness of the controls. The process can be documented in a Word format or as a visual presentation through flowcharts. An experienced reviewer, such as the internal audit department, would then typically be able to identify the potential weaknesses in the business process.

Whereas a complete segregation of all potentially conflicting duties might only reasonably be achievable in a large operation, compensating controls further on in the process might be effective in mitigating the perceived weakness earlier in the process. For example, where the available headcount in the purchases department is limited such that the same individual is required to create a vendor, issue purchase orders and reconcile the supplier statements, design effectiveness might still be achieved by ensuring that the receipting is independent and that the request for payment is appropriately scrutinised prior to authorisation.

Monitoring Controls

In **Chapter 7**, we discussed the various methods available to monitor whether the controls operate as designed (their design effectiveness) as well as for the whole period under review (their operating effectiveness). Management should then separately track the findings and issues that arise from the monitoring of the operational effectiveness of the fraud controls as well as their resolution. In particular, management should be vigilant for instances of possible collusion between control owners to circumvent properly designed segregation of duties. Alternatively, management might be required to introduce additional training to ensure that the control owners fully appreciate what is expected from them. In cases of serious or continuous failures, disciplinary procedures might be considered against the relevant control owners.

The findings from the monitoring activities would typically also provide a useful reference point for the next fraud risk assessment when management have to determine the appropriateness of its strategies and controls. For example, management might be required to introduce additional compensating controls of review and oversight at the corporate level in instances where the results of the business unit-level controls were unsatisfactory.

Aggregating Fraud Risks

Because the fraud risk assessment is driven top-down from corporate management, rather than bottom-up from local management, there is no need to aggregate the individual risk maps from the business units. In fact, local management should be discouraged from disaggregating the central risk map and thereby, perhaps inadvertently, reducing the significance of a particular fraud risk.

It might, however, be useful to prepare risk templates for each of the fraud risks so as to compare and contrast the effectiveness of the various responses from each of the business units. Therefore, this phase falls after the controlling fraud risk phase, which is a slight deviation from the phases of the enterprise risk management process.

Residual Fraud Risk Map

After the completion of the monitoring of the operating effectiveness of the fraud controls, the residual risk map should be prepared. The audit committee of the board of directors might be particularly interested in understanding the remaining or residual level of fraud risk after taking into account the various controls and procedures designed to prevent and detect prohibited activities.

The risk items on the residual fraud risk map should generally move diagonally downwards, towards the green (or lightly shaded) sectors of the risk map, on the basis of effectively designed controls. However, where properly designed controls do not operate as intended and for the entire period expected, their overall effectiveness would be significantly reduced. In such circumstances, the relative position on the residual fraud risk map might be unchanged from that of the inherent risk map. Management can therefore assess the quality of the controls on the ground, based on this relative movement. Ultimately, the board should determine whether the result from the residual fraud risk map is in keeping with the overall risk appetite of the organisation.

Updating Fraud Risks

As discussed before, an organisation might generally consider a biannual fraud risk assessment as being sufficiently frequent. This aims to strike a balance between a rapidly changing business environment on the one hand and providing enough time to gather and digest relevant information on the other. The delay in time is also necessary to ensure that senior management approach the assessment with renewed focus and so avoid 'assessment-fatigue' setting in. Management would also have gained further insights during the intervening six months into the potential exposure to fraud from the nature of the allegations reported through the hotline and the findings from the resultant investigations. This experience should serve to continuously inform whether the current controls are still designed and operating effectively and thereby significantly enhance the overall efficacy of the fraud programme.

Also, by revisiting this area in a systematic and frequent manner, the correct 'tone at the top' is established and reinforced. It will be clearly established throughout the organisation that management take the continuous prevention and detection of fraud very seriously.

Legislation

In April 2009, the UK Bribery Act was passed into law, although not yet enacted. It creates a general offence related to both the payment ('active') and receipt ('passive') of bribes within and outside of the United Kingdom. Senior managers that consent or connive with such activities would also be guilty of an offence.

Importantly, a new offence (analogous to some of the clauses contained in the US Foreign Corrupt Practices Act) in respect of the negligent failure to prevent active bribery is also created. In order to avail of a defence against this offence, a UK organisation would need to prove that it had already implemented adequate procedures in this respect.

Although 'adequate procedures' are undefined in the Act, the following components would normally be expected in this regard:

- overall guidelines and principles (such as the general definition of fraud and prohibitions contained in the code of conduct or fraud policy);
- customised responses and procedures (such as those flowing from the above described bi-annual fraud risk assessments); and
- implementation of the fraud programme (such as the fraud investigations and monitoring of the effectiveness of the fraud-related controls).

Organisations should, therefore, carefully consider whether their existing fraud prevention practices are robust enough to qualify as 'adequate procedures'.

Conclusion

In this chapter we considered the various aspects of the risk assessment process that an organisation can adopt in response to the pervasive threat of fraud. In the next and final chapter, we will focus on some of the challenges and barriers facing an organisation that wishes to implement an enterprise risk management programme.

Chapter 10

Challenges and Barriers

Introduction

In the previous chapters we have discussed the infrastructure required in implementing an enterprise risk management programme as well as how to respond to specific topics such as disaster recovery and fraud. In this chapter we will focus on the various challenges and barriers that an organisation might encounter when rolling out these programmes.

The Expectation Gap

In **Chapter 2**, we mentioned the important caveat that any enterprise risk management programme, and by extension any corporate governance model, is ultimately dependent on the quality of the individuals involved. If the aim of the programme is to share accurate information concerning risks in a timely manner with the correct level of management, then the appropriateness of their responses is still dependent on the competence of management.

Human decision-making abilities are invariably hampered by inexperience associated with having to deal with completely new issues, on the one hand, and prejudices resulting from experience dealing with previous or related issues, on the other. The UK model of corporate governance attempts, for example, to overcome this by placing emphasis on the segregation of the role of chairman and managing director at the top of the organisation, the idea being that the collective wisdom and insight of both these individuals ought to balance or enhance each other and thereby produce better results over time.

The gathering of complete and accurate information is another significant challenge. Management can ultimately not be expected to take the appropriate action if they are unaware of the issue. Similarly, if the issue is only communicated once it has crystallized, then the options open to management might be limited. We have described in **Chapter 6** how these aspects of the enterprise risk management programme can be continuously refined and improved. We noted that frequent (re)assessments involving a broad range of participants, coupled with consistent, succinct communications, should yield the best results over time.

In particular, the effectiveness of the programme is greatly enhanced where local management have 'bought into' it. We will consider in the next section of this chapter some of the possible reasons why local management would be reluctant to fully engage.

It is important that the board of directors understand these inherent limitations associated with both corporate governance and enterprise risk management. Although no system can ever provide absolute assurances, a properly designed and monitored structure should provide reasonable comfort that risks are being identified, communicated and appropriate actions are being taken as a result. That does not remove the requirement of eternal vigilance from the board.

Engagement from Local Management

At some level all organisations are constantly engaged in risk mitigation procedures. The focus of enterprise risk management is to provide a consistent framework to document and assess the risks and related strategies and controls.

Management might be reluctant to engage in the process for the following perceived reasons:

- 'Big Brother' intrusion by the corporate head office;
- unreasonable curtailment of the independence of business unit management;
- unnecessary duplication of effort/bureaucratic;
- binary nature of conclusions; or
- no value-add.

'Big Brother'

In certain organisations the culture or ethos is such that a significant level of autonomy or independence is bestowed on the management team of the individual business units. The corporate head offices of such organisations are usually small in terms of headcount as well as in their narrowly-defined authority. This structure is not necessarily inappropriate, provided that the main board is satisfied that the overall risks and exposures taken by the individual business units are in keeping with the group risk appetite.

Where the corporate head office intends to roll out an enterprise risk management programme (as outlined in **Chapters 6** and **7**), the local business units might consider this an unwelcome and unwarranted intrusion on their independence and indeed their competence.

In response to this concern, the board might consider whether to limit the scope of the enterprise risk management programme to primarily focus on identifying only those risks that could have a significant group- or organisation-wide impact, rather than cataloguing all relevant risks and responses at each business unit. Similarly, the input from the corporate head office to the strategies and controls adopted by local management to address these key risks would typically be limited to advice, rather than enforcing standardised best practices across the organisation. Furthermore, the monitoring of the operational effectiveness of the controls might be specifically restricted to self-certification from local management, instead of using, say, an internal audit function to provide independent comfort and assurance.

However, as we have discussed, the board must consider whether this 'toned-down' or 'light-touch' approach is still appropriate given not only the organisation's internal risk appetite, but also the complete regulatory regime in which it operates.

Curtailment

Similar to the 'intrusion' concerns outlined above, local management might consider that corporate management are simply too far removed from their own specific businesses such that the structure brought by an enterprise risk management programme might be too restrictive. Local management might determine that this level of corporate oversight in particular places unacceptable impediment and restrictions on their entrepreneurial flair.

Such concerns could be addressed through the careful design of the authority matrix. Consistent again with the risk appetite of the organisation, the approval levels might be set at relatively high monetary levels to allow local management to have most of their required independence. Put another way, the 'box' or structure in which the business unit should be conducting its activities can be as large as it needs to be.

However, the disciplines of an enterprise risk management programme are still critical in first determining what the sides of the 'box' are. Otherwise, the board of directors cannot reasonably consider which of the local business unit activities should fall outside of their close oversight. The shape of the 'box' (or, more precisely, the nature of circumscribed activities and monetary ceilings) is of course specifically linked and tied into the culture and riskiness of the organisation and the type of businesses and markets in which it operates.

The enterprise risk management programme can be 'tweaked' in such a predetermined manner as to provide only the tools for determining the shape and size of the 'box' in which the local business units have to operate. Neither corporate management nor the board would necessarily then be concerned with the effectiveness of the controls and strategies adopted by local management, provided that the activities or monetary ceilings are not breached. The monitoring phase would be limited to ensuring that the occasional activities outside of the 'box' are reported to the corporate head office in a timely manner.

Clearly, such a tweaking of the risk management phases would remove the possibility and benefits of establishing best practices across the organisation as well as the ultimate effectiveness of the overall risk management programme. However, the board of directors might determine that this 'lite' programme is in keeping with their risk management philosophy.

Duplication of Effort

At some level, mitigation of risk typically takes place at all business units all the time. One of the normal responsibilities of management is, indeed, stewardship of the equity invested in each business unit, which clearly requires a measure of risk management. This may range from detailed procedures such as credit checking potential customers at one end to considering multi-year business strategy proposals at the other.

In some cases local management might have formally documented their strategies and controls developed in order to mitigate the risks they had identified. In such circumstances, local management might therefore reasonably consider that engaging in the formalised processes of an enterprise risk management would be an unnecessary duplication of effort. The board of directors, on the other hand, might be equally concerned that local management have focussed only on the particular risks that they consider important to their own businesses, or might have missed significant risks altogether. The local business unit risk registers would therefore not necessarily align with the risks applicable and important to the overall group.

In response to these concerns, the board might determine that the information gathering process is most effectively conducted through personal interviews at the business units rather than the circulation of questionnaires from the corporate head office. In **Chapter 6** we have already discussed some of the other benefits and drawbacks of the various methods for identifying risk. In particular, the risk management department should normally be tasked with the documentation and maintenance of the information so as to minimise the administrative burden on local management associated with the implementation of the programme.

An equally important task of the risk management department or function is to leverage off as much as possible from what has already been created by local management. Although there are clear benefits to the consistency conventions brought about by the enterprise risk management programme, the operational effectiveness of the controls and strategies are ultimately of more importance. It is therefore not necessary to reinvent the existing control environment at each business unit just to ensure conformity. Instead, best practices and recommendations can be shared, but only mandated where the existing controls are found not to be sufficiently robust. Throughout the enterprise risk management programme it is therefore necessary to periodically engage with local management to ensure that only those critical recommendations are included in the risk report.

Another area where leverage and, therefore, cost saving might be realised is in the reliance placed on the enterprise risk management programme by external auditors. In **Chapter 7** we discussed how the verification procedures might be aligned to the methodologies of the external auditors. As their standards on auditing require them to perform risk identification, walkthroughs and, where appropriate, control testing, that work might be conducted for the direct benefit of both the external audit and local management. Such sharing of benefits might in certain circumstance result in a saving in audit fees.

The above suggestions should help to limit the amount of resources and time required from local management whilst at the same time ensuring the significant group risks and key weaknesses are adequately addressed.

Binary Conclusions

In **Chapter 5**, which dealt with the format and layout of risk reports, we indicated that an over-emphasis on the ultimate rating attached to the control environment of a business unit might undermine the detailed conclusions and recommendations. The readers of the report, ranging from the board of directors at the one end to local management at the other, might incorrectly determine that a 'strong/good' rating is sufficient to conclude that all the other detailed recommendations made are either optional or, at best, 'nice-to-haves'. Similarly, local management might be more focussed on ensuring that the rating falls within a pre-determined acceptable bracket, than in responding to individual weaknesses and developing a credible roadmap to address the recommendations made.

It is therefore important, as part of the roll-out of the enterprise risk management programme, to educate the various readers of the risk reports to attach the correct relative weighting to the overall rating given. The board should be significantly more focussed on the nature of all the recommendations and whether any trends might be distilled from the frequency of their occurrence. The risk management department should also invest time upfront to ensure that local management understand the format of the risk report and its intended audience. Furthermore, it is important to limit the report to a small number of pages so as to ensure that the intended audience is able to work through its entirety, rather than perhaps just reading the executive summary.

The board might determine that the format of the risk report should not include any overall ratings so as to avoid the issues outline above. However, where there are a large number of individually small business units, it might not be necessary and desirable to maintain these ratings.

Finally, the conclusions and rating from the enterprise risk management report should not be used as part of the measures to calculate salary increases or bonuses for senior management of the related business unit. The purpose of the risk report is to provide the board of directors and local management with an overview of how risk is being managed at each business unit and the organisation overall. Balanced scorecards and broad performance measurement programmes are the tools organisations typically use to determine remuneration levels instead.

Value Add

The risk report can be seen as mainly the culmination and systematic documentation of the interviews with various members on local management where independent monitoring of the controls has not been scoped in. Local management might, therefore, contend that the risk report does not add any value as it only reflects what has already been known.

This contention ignores the broader organisation and its other stakeholders. A key part of the enterprise risk management programme is to provide the correct information to the correct levels of management in a timely manner. The board of directors might not necessarily be as familiar with the risks of each individual business unit and would therefore consider that a consistent and formalised approach to this information gathering adds value to their fiduciary duties and decision-making processes.

Local management, on the other hand, might also benefit from the risk reports, especially in the sharing of best practices from other business units from across the organisation. For example, broader strategies on how to be successful in specific markets or jurisdictions might be shared internally without having to be recreated by different business units within the same organisation. In very large organisations, the risk management department might then almost be seen as the keeper of a central information depository or part of the knowledge management system.

Of course local management might also benefit from the collective wisdom and insight of the organisation in order to respond to specific risks instead of having to rely exclusively on their own experiences.

Conclusion

In this chapter we outlined some of the limitations inherent in any enterprise risk management programme. We also discussed some of the objections that are typically raised against head office oversight, in general, and enterprise risk management, in particular, together with some suggested responses.

Ultimately though, it is important to note that the implementation of enterprise risk management is a significant programme that would most likely result in some level of disruption to the business units of the organisation. It is, however, equally important to note the huge potential benefits that such a programme would bring to the organisation as a whole. It is, as with all risk management strategies, the responsibility of those charged with the governance of the organisation to ensure that these rewards outweigh the risks.

INDEX

Accepting risk, 72, *see* **Risk management process**
  Corporate risk appetite, 73–75, *see also* **Control infrastructure**
  Future risks, 77, 88
  Interaction with existing risks, 76
  Potential risks, 77
  Source of risks, 75
Aggregating risk, 56, *see* **Risk Management process**
  Overall risk maps, 82
  Overall risk register, 78, 82–84, *see also* **Risk register**
  Risk template, 79–82
    Analysis of responses, 80
    Example of, 80, 81
    Headings in, 79
    Overall conclusions, 80
    Risk description, 79
    Risk item and name, 79
  Sub-organisational aggregation, 84
Avoidable risks, 15, 77, *see also* **Risks**
  Causes of, 76
  Classification of, 73
  Likelihood of, 76
  Types of, 15
  Unacceptable, 73

'Big bang approach', 41, *see* **Risk management process**

Codes of conduct, 20
  Beyond codes, 24
    Certification, 24
    Communication from senior executives, 24
    Dedicated ethic programme, 25
    Feedback channels, 25

150   *Enterprise Risk Management*

    Frequently asked questions, 24
    Training courses, 24
  Fraud, 25, *see* **Fraud**
  Level of detail in, 20
  Nature of, 20
  Principles based codes, 20
    Example of, 21
  Rules based codes, 21–23
    Example of, 22
Communication, 42, *see also* **Organisational structures**
  Maintaining of, 42
  Open, 42
  Report to directors,
    Detailed supporting schedules, 45
    Executive summary, 43, 44
    Outline of approach, 44
Controls, *see also* **Control infrastructure**, **Fraud** and **Strategies**
  Allocating, 94
    Amber sector risks, 95
    Green sector risk items, 94
    Red sector risks, 95
  Monitoring of, 103
    Certifications, 103
    Internal audit, 27, 106–108
    Questionnaires, 52–54, 104
    Reliance on work of others, 108
    Risk management department, 39, 56, 106
    Self-assessments, 54, 105
  Walkthroughs of, 100–103, 136
Control infrastructure, *see also* **Controls**
  Codes of conduct, *see* **Codes of Conduct**
  Fraud policy, 25–28, *see also* **Fraud**
    Alternate processes and, 27
      Ad hoc investigation team, 27
      Internal audit, 27, 106–108
      Outside specialist, 28
      Senior management, 28
  Group/company policies, 32–36
    Accounting polices, 33

Authorisation matrix, 33–35
    Example of, 34
Employee handbooks, 32
Terms of reference, 35, 36
Reporting mechanisms, 28, *see also* **Fraud** and **Reporting mechanisms**

Corporate governance, 4–9
Combined Code on Corporate Governance, 4, 6
Concept of, 4
Listed companies and
Principles of, 4, 5
Scope of, 5

Corporate vision statement, 17, 73
Corporate strategies, 18
    Types of, 18
Example of, 17, 18
Performance management programmes, 19
Tactical responses, 19

Disaster recovery,
Meaning of, 110
Plan,
    Activating, 112
    Administration of, 111
    Considerations of, 111
    Maintenance of, 111
Scenario planning, 117
    Computer virus, 123, 124
    Flooding, 118–120
    Gas explosion, 120–122
    Infectious disease, 122, 123
Team,
    Command centre, 114
    Communications team, 116
    Facilities team, 116
    Human resources team, 117
    Information technology team, 114
    Members of, 113
    Team leader, 113

Employee handbooks, 32
Enterprise risk management,
  Definition of, 5, 6
  Goal of, 6
  Scope of, 7–9
Ethics, 24, 25, *see also* **Codes of Conduct**
  Dedicated programme of, 25
  Independent programme of, 125
Executive sponsorship, 37, *see also* **Organisational structures**
  Benefits of, 37
  Implementation of, 37
  Owner of the process, 37
  Rationale for, 37
External risks, 13, 14, *see also* **Risks**
  Impact of, 57, 66
  Numbering of, 57
  Types of, 13, 57
  Likelihood of, 14, 57, 68

Fraud, *see also* **Codes of Conduct, Control, Control infrastructure** and **Fraud Policy**
  Definition of, 125–127
  Investigations, 129
  Legislation and, 139
  Policy, 25, 127
  Reporting mechanisms, 127
  Risk assessment, 58, 129
    Accepting fraud risks, 132
    Aggregating fraud risks, 137
    Allocating controls, 134
      Board of directors, 134
      Business unit management, 135
      Corporate management, 135
      Segregation of duties, 135
    Controlling fraud risks, 132
      Corruption, 134
      Falsification frauds, 133
      Financial statement frauds, 132
      Misappropriation frauds, 133

Grading of fraud risks, 132
Identification of fraud risks,
    130–132
Monitoring controls, 137
Residual fraud risk map, 138
Updating fraud risks, 138
   Segregation of duties and, 31, 125
   Training certifications, 128
   Training programmes, 128
Fraud policy, 25–28, *see also* **Fraud**
   Alternate processes and, 27
      Ad hoc investigation team, 27
      Internal audit, 27, 106–108
      Outside specialist, 28
      Senior management, 28
   Definition of, 26
   Example of, 26
Future risks, 73, *see also* **Risks**
   Acceptance of, 77
   Avoiding of, 77, 78
   Assessment of, 15

Hybrid risks, 14, 57, *see also* **Risks**
   Examples of, 57
   Impact of, 68
   Numbering system and, 57
   Response to, 14
   Strategies and, 86

Internal Audit department, *see also* **Organisational
       structures**
   Remit of, 38
   Procedures of, 38
   Focus of, 38
   Test plans of, 38
Internal risks, 13, 14, *see also* **Risks**
   Acceptance of, 75
   Controls and, 85
   Impact of, 68

Likelihood of, 68
Management programmes and, 40
Sub-stratification plan and, 57
Type of, 14, 57
Irish Stock Exchange
Corporate governance and, 4, *see also* **Corporate Governance**

Legal and compliance department, 38, *see also* **Organisational structures**
Focus of, 38
Legislation, 126
Changes in, 57
Fraud and, 3, 139, *see* **Fraud**
London Stock Exchange
Corporate governance and, 4, *see also* **Corporate Governance**

Organisational structures,
Communication, 42–45, *see* **Communication**
Decentralised model, 40
Executive sponsorship, 37
Finance department, 39
Internal audit department, 38
Legal and compliance department, 38
Risk management department, 39, 56, 106, *see also* **Controls** and **Control infrastructures**
Recommendations, 45
   Documentation matters, 47
   Limited changes, 47
   Significant changes, 47
Roll out of the process, 41
   Pilot schemes, 41

Pension schemes, 46, 81
Control of, 62
Deficit in defined, 65, 81
   Hybrid risk as, 57, *see also* **Hybrid risks**
Validity of assumptions used in pension models, 58, 61, 135

Recession, 1, 131
   Global, 57, 66, 67, 86, 87, 96
   Impact of, 131, 132
   Response to, 63
   Domestic, 15, 57, 66, 67, 86, 87, 96
Regulations,
   Breaches of, 29
   Changes in, 57
   Compliance with, 38
   Industry specific, 15
Reporting mechanisms, 28, *see also* **Fraud** and **Reporting mechanisms**
   Confidential helpline, 30
   Reporting to an independent department, 29
   Reporting to direct line management, 29
   Organisational charts, 31, 32
   Suggestion boxes, 31
Risks *see* **Risk management process** and **Risk register**
   Categories of, 13
     Response types, 13, 57
       External risk, 13, 57, *see* **External risks**
       Internal risk, 14, 57, *see* **Internal risks**
       Hybrid risks, 14, 57, *see* **Hybrid risks**
     Risk appetite,
       Avoidable risks, 15, 72, *see* **Avoidable risks**
       Future risks, 15, 72, 77, *see* **Future risks**
       Unavoidable risks, 15, 72, *see* **Unavoidable risks**
   Chance, 11
     Likelihood, 11, 65
     Impact, 11, 12, 65
   Definition of, 10, 49
   Emerging risks, 15
   Mitigation of, 45, 85–89, 110–124, *see also* **Controls** *and* **Disaster recovery**
     Amber risks, 46, 95
     Green risks, 46, 94
     Red risks, 46, 95
   Interaction between risks, 16

156 *Enterprise Risk Management*

    Process of managing, *see* **Risk management process**
    Upside, 12
    Updating, 48, 89–93, 138
Risk Management Department, 39, *see also* **Organisational structures**
    Function of, 39
    Monitoring of compliance, 39
    Role of, 39
    Size of, 40
Risk management process, 41
    Accepting risk, 72, *see* **Accepting risk**
    Aggregating risk, 56, *see* **Aggregating risk**
    Challenges to, 141–148
        Engagement from local management
            'big brother', 142
            Binary conclusions, 146
            Curtailment, 143
            Duplication of effort, 144–146
            Value add, 147
        Expectation gap, 141
    Controlling risk, 85
        Categories,
            Controls, 85
            Design effectiveness, 87
            Potential risks, 88
            Strategies, 86
    Grading risk, 63
        Impact, 11, 12, 65
        Inherent risks, 67
        Likelihood, 11, 65
        Relative grading approach, 66
        Residual risk, 67–69
        Risk maps, 64
            Final residual, 71
            Initial residual, 69, 70
            Overall, 82–84
    Identifying risk, 49
        Corporate head office, 62

      Gathering information, 52
         Direct interviews, 55
         Questionnaires, 52–54, 104
         Self-assessments, 54
      Number of risks identified, 60
      Potential risks, 62
      Risk and control matrix, 61
      Scoping, 50–52
   Stages of, 49–93
   Updating risks,
      Embedding the process, 90
      Re-assessment process, 91–93
      Wrap-up, 89

Risk register, 56, 72, *see also* **Risks** and **Risk management process**
   External risk, 13, 57
   Financial integrity risks, 58
   Fraud risks, 58
   Human resource risks, 59
   Hybrid risks, 14, 57
   Information risks, 59
   Internal risk, 14, 57
   Legal risks, 58
   Operational risks, 59
   Overall, 78, 79
   Reputational risks, 59
   Strategic risks, 58, *see also* **Strategies**

Strategies, *see also* **Controls** and **Control infrastructures**
   Tracking, 95
      Budgets, 98
         Discounted cash flow, 98, 99
      Individual matters, 96
      Project sponsor/manager, 100
      Setting overall goals, 96

Strengths, Weaknesses, Opportunities and Threats ('SWOT') analysis, 15

Taxation,
   Budgeted profit before tax, 12
      Scoping and, 51
   Computation of corporate tax charge, 107
   Tax implications when changing to a single entity, 97
Turnbull Guidance, 6, 29

Unavoidable risks, 15, 72, *see also* **Risks**
   Types of, 15